C000200979

Le Coq Hardi

Le Coq Hardi

The Story of John Howard
and His Restaurant

Michael O'Sullivan
Illustrated by Melinda Patton

BLACKWATER PRESS

Editor
Antoinette Walker

Design & Layout
Melanie Gradtke

Illustrations
Melinda Patton

Cover Design
Melanie Gradtke

© Michael O'Sullivan, 2003

ISBN 1-84131-635-0

Printed in Ireland by Blackwater Press, c/o Folens Publishers, Hibernian Industrial Estate, Greenhills Road, Tallaght, Dublin 24

"My Father's Cellar" by Auberon Waugh on pages 96–101 was first published by Berry Bros. and Rudd in *Number Three, St James's Street,* 1986.

All rights reserved. No part of this publication may be reproduced or transmitted in any form or by any means electronic, mechanical, photocopying, recording, or otherwise without the prior permission of the Publisher.

This book is sold subject to the conditions that it shall not, by way of trade or otherwise, be lent, re-sold, hired out or otherwise circulated without the Publisher's consent in any form or cover other than that in which it is published and without similar conditions, including this condition being imposed on the subsequent purchaser.

For five dear friends –
John and Valli Murray Brown, Gillian Mcnaughton,
Julian Pearson and Petroc Trelawny

Acknowledgements

The author wishes to thank John, Catherine and Karen Howard for answering the many queries with which they were bombarded during the writing of this book. It was read in manuscript by Zeynep Asya and by Valli Murray Brown, who both made valuable improvements and suggestions. John Corless provided much useful information and supported the project from the beginning. Stephen J. Quinn of Sovern Hotels gave moral support and much needed encouragement and advice. Tadgh Geary of Pallas Foods gave generously of his knowledge of the food industry in Ireland, as did Patrick Clement of Pallas Foods.

The author also wishes to thank Derek Clarke, Jane Williams, Desmond FitzGerald, Knight of Glin, Margaret Hyland, John Heather, Philip McMaster, and Anne Henderson of the Irish Architectural Archive.

For permission to reproduce photographic images, the following are gratefully acknowledged: Alamy Images, Camera Press Ireland/Colman Doyle, Finnegan Menton, Jason Clarke Photography, National Photographic Archive, Richard Beere, and The Irish Times Picture Library. Grateful thanks are also extended to Lady Teresa Waugh and Berry Bros. and Rudd for permission to reproduce "My Father's Cellar" by Auberon Waugh.

Finally, a special word of thanks to the editor of the book, Antoinette Walker, for her support and consummate skill in seeing the book through to the QED.

Contents

Introduction

There is no love sincerer than the love of food.
George Bernard Shaw

*O*f the many things that contribute to defining a great city, one must surely be the longevity of its restaurants. In this respect, Dublin ranks sadly behind its European neighbours. With the exception of the dining rooms of the Shelbourne and Gresham hotels, the city can offer neither native nor visitor many restaurants with a long history. It has not always been so.

Quite a few great Dublin restaurants survived the vicissitudes visited on them by rebellion, world wars and civil war. Few, however, survived the profound change in taste wrought on the capital by the new affluence, which was in place by the 1970s. Some of the culinary legends of the past teetered on or were by then mere memories.

At the end of the nineteenth century, Corless' restaurant on Grafton Street was one of the grandest and most fashionable in Dublin. It was a favourite haunt of the aristocracy and renowned for the quality of its oysters. Its owner, Thomas Corless, came from a prosperous Galway family and was the confidant of most of the fashionable people of the day. Mr Corless' daughter was an accomplished soprano and delighted patrons with the occasional aria, delivered without accompaniment in the restaurant's spacious rooms. James Joyce, when he came to publish *Ulysses* in 1922, recalled that it was Corless' restaurant that became the legendary Jammet's.

Jammet's, founded by Lord Cadogan's chef in 1900, was a worthy successor to Mr Corless' establishment. It was, in its day, the most celebrated of Dublin's eating establishments. It closed its doors in 1967. Jammet's famous rooms, with their murals of the four seasons, was situated at the Trinity end of Grafton Street in the building where Dublin's most exclusive night club, Lillie's, is now situated. All these grand dames of Irish gastronomy had, mercifully, surrendered their tiaras to the vaults of memory by the time MacDonalds opened its doors on Grafton Street in May 1977.

By an odd coincidence, that same year, an Irish gastronomic legend in the making opened its doors in suburban Ballsbridge. *Le Coq Hardi* quickly became the flagship for a new form of culinary excellence in a rapidly changing Dublin. It embraced some of the better characteristics of the old restaurants, and offered the new generation something to claim as their own. They too, in their turn, have become sentimental about its demise, much as their parents and grand-

The Dolphin Hotel

parents did about Jammet's, the Russell, the Moira, the Dolphin, the Royal Hibernan, and the Red Bank.

The Seventies in Dublin began with tension and unrest in Northern Ireland dominating the political scene. One of *Le Coq Hardi's* future patrons, Minister for Finance, Charles Haughey, was arrested and charged with involvement in an alleged attempt to import arms illegally into the Republic. As the seventies opened, Ireland was still very much dependent on its close economic relationship with Britain. That, as so much else, would change somewhat after accession to the EEC in 1973. The Seventies in Ireland bore all the hallmarks of the "low dishonest decade" that W.H. Auden had dubbed another earlier period elsewhere.

However, in Ireland one thing was quite different. With the death of de Valera's ideal Eden, the country embraced ostentatious consumption as few others in Europe did. All the old shibboleths were being attacked. The special constitutional protection afforded the Roman Catholic Church was removed; Mary Robinson began her crusade to legalise contraception; the special position of the Irish language disappeared and the Archbishop of Dublin decreed that it was no longer a mortal sin for Catholics to attend Trinity College Dublin.

In the Seventies, Archbishop John Charles McQuaid also consecrated that former bastion of sybaritic hedonism in D'Olier Street, the Red Bank Restaurant, into a Sacred Heart chapel for the daily exposition of the Blessed Sacrament. Here the citizens of Dublin could seek expiation, at a less secular altar, than that which previously was obtained in the building.

In a sense the Seventies in Ireland was the decade of Jack Lynch. His massive parliamentary majority won at the 1977 General Election set the tone for the period. Everything was for sale, or at least had a price. In purchasing the votes of the electorate, the administration engulfed the country in a form of disastrous economic suicide, which it was still paying for ten years later. The feel-good factor induced by this form of political lunacy fuelled spending in clubs and restaurants. It was in the atmosphere, if not the detail, of these events that John and Catherine Howard opened *Le Coq Hardi* in March 1977.

1 From Ballyvaughan to the Café Royal

We may live without poetry, music and art;
We may live without conscience, and
Live without heart;
We may live without friends, we may
Live without books;
But civilised man cannot live without
Cooks.

The Earl of Lyton
Poet and Diplomat

*T*he story of *Le Coq Hardi* begins not in the fashionable Dublin suburb of Ballsbridge, but on the western seaboard of Ireland, near the picturesque County Clare village of Ballyvaughan. John Howard was born there on 5 December 1945, the first son of Patrick and Johanna Howard. The omens for a future restaurateur and wine lover read well. The year 1945 was, arguably, one of the greatest vintage years.

A late medieval settlement predates the present village of Ballyvaughan. It witnessed a bitter feud in 1540 over that most Irish of disputes – a stolen cow. It survived this turbulent moment, as it did an attack by the forces of Sir Henry Sydney, to become a tranquil fishing village noted for its excellent herrings and thriving oyster beds.

Ballyvaughan briefly enjoyed the status of capital of northwest Clare. It was one of the first villages in Ireland to have a reliable public water system that successfully coaxed gravity to carry the supply in cast-iron pipes. A village fountain commemorates those benefactors whose munificent foresight saw the system installed. Today the village is the centre of a busy tourist trail. Its proximity to the natural beauty of the spectacular limestone Burren region guarantees its future.

Just a year before John Howard was born, the Aillwee caves were discovered outside Ballyvaughan. A local farmer stumbled by accident on the two million-year-old natural phenomenon. Another natural wonder, Corkscrew Hill, is nearby as is the evidence of prehistoric activity in a *fulacht fiadh* or cooking place. With a hill named after a corkscrew and a prehistoric oven as the twin backdrops to his place of birth, it seemed that the omens were all auspicious for Ballyvaughan to give birth to one of Ireland's most famous chefs.

The period was characterised by wartime food rationing. The ration system was controlled by Seán Lemass who was given the thankless task of heading up the Ministry of Supplies. "The Emergency", as the war was known in neutral Ireland, placed its own particular constraints on her citizens intake of life's necessities and luxuries. For a nation of tea drinkers, one of the most onerous deprivations was the rationing of the "vital oolong", as P.G. Wodehouse put it. The allowance of half an ounce a week drove tea addicts to strange and desperate efforts of compensation. Attempts were made to brew tea from dandelion leaves, and coffee from, of all things, rhubarb. Children were given mashed parsnip sandwiches as a substitute for the banana. Citrus fruit was an unknown quantity.

Ballyvaughan by William Lawrence

In the midst of all this sensory deprivation there were reports of well-heeled foreign visitors coming to Dublin to dine on the magnificent fish and beef offered at Jammet's. Some of those visitors were German internees from Irish detention camps. German airmen who had strayed onto Irish soil were often received with a hearty Irish welcome and, altogether, had a very good war.

Dublin on VE Day, 8 May 1945, did not witness the joyous celebrations seen elsewhere. As the conflict in Europe ended, families whose sons had fought with the British Army were relieved or saddened, according to their loved one's fate. The students of Trinity College flew the Union Jack from the West Front of that ancient seat of learning and burned the Irish Tricolour at the entrance gate to the college. In retaliation students from University College Dublin burned a Union Jack outside Trinity and jeered at the Trinitymen waving the Union Flag in further provocation. One of the UCD students was Charles Haughey, a future Taoiseach and perhaps one of the most famous future patrons of *Le Coq Hardi.* Minor rioting followed in which the windows of Jammet's restaurant were smashed. At the time, Trinity had a large proportion of English public schoolmen and Anglo-Irish on its books, many of whom would have been loyal to the ideals of Empire.

John Howard was born into a rather different world. His parents farmed a small holding at Fermoyle outside Ballyvaughan. The family, like so many others at the time, was essentially self-sufficient. Beef, pork, milk, butter, eggs, fruit and vegetables were all produced on the farm. Pork was pickled and the excess sold in Ballyvaughan. On the nearby bog at Mount Elva, the young Howard cut turf with his father. In many respects, his upbringing conformed to the ideals of rustic bliss put forward by de Valera.

John and his brothers Patrick and Peter Joseph all attended the local national school. John walked the three and a half miles from the family farm to school in the morning and the same distance back in the afternoon. Later, John was sent to the secondary school run by the Sisters of Mercy in Lisdoonvarna. This Clare spa town and resort is famous for lonely hearts seeking companions and for the ill seeking a miraculous cure in its sulphur-laden waters.

During his time at the school, he lodged with Joe and Una Lynam in their guesthouse. It was here that he engaged in his first professional outing as a chef. Some guests arrived one evening when the Lynams were out visiting.

Having been admitted by the young Howard, they asked if they might have something to eat. With all the certitude of the future award-winning chef, he tackled the task and served his first meal to the first of his many satisfied customers. He recalled that his mother's cooking at home had little or no influence on him. "Cabbage," he once told a friend "was put on to cook before we went out to Mass and it was deemed to be ready for consumption by the time we arrived home."

Simple fare was the order of the day. Fatty bacon, pork, fresh fish and potatoes were the staples of the farming household when John was growing up. Most farmers' wives were very good bakers and soda bread and sweet cakes were supplements to the more mundane things on offer.

Apart from the occasional turn as a guest chef at Lynam's, John also supplemented his income as a signwriter. His handiwork was still visible until recently over Hynes's sweet shop overlooking Lisdoonvarna's world-famous sulphur baths.

During school vacations, recreation was a simple matter of local sports. John played hurling and was an avid supporter of the local and county teams. He remembers the Clare hurling legends Jimmy Smith and Paddy Cronin playing for Clare. Indeed, he followed the county team through all their vicissitudes until victory in an All-Ireland final came their way in 1995.

Though he later encountered some of the most famous and infamous politicians in the land, John showed no interest in politics as a young man. The family played no leading role in the independence movement, but it supported De Valera who had made County Clare his political base.

By the time John left school, County Clare was beginning to benefit from the development of Shannon Airport. It was in the year of his birth, 1945, that the government secured the agreement for all eastbound traffic from the United States to stop there. Soon a new town sprang up to serve the airport and a growing customs-free industrial zone.

A catering college was also established at Shannon and it was there that John Howard began his professional training in 1960. He recalled that the emphasis at the college was on the classical French cooking for which he would later make his reputation in *Le Coq Hardi*. His mentors were chefs Andre Trevaud and Willie Ryan, who taught him his early skills.

It was the era of the great showbands. Rural dancehalls resounded to that primal cry of "keep 'em sweatin'". John recalls quite a social buzz at Shannon that witnessed the comings and goings of various shades of celebrity. The eponymous dish is a rarity in Ireland and those that do exist seem to have their origin at airports. Irish Coffee was invented at Shannon when that legendary elixir Tullamore Dew, invented by D.E. Williams of Tullamore, was added to coffee, sugar and cream. Pancakes Colleen was invented at Dublin airport. This dish was named after Colleen Stafford whose family owned the Gresham Hotel in Dublin and The Talbot in Wexford. The catering manager at Shannon, Paddy McMahon, was a relative of John Howard by marriage. The McMahon's owned much of the land around Shannon and John lodged with them for the three years he was a student at the catering college.

In 1963, John took his first step towards becoming a professional chef when he joined the staff of the Waldorf Hotel on Dublin's Eden Quay. Here he came under the influence of head chef, Liam Riddler, who came from a well-known Limerick family of chefs. His brother, Michael Riddler, was head chef at the Glentworth Hotel in Limerick City. The charms of the little-known Dublin Waldorf did not hold John's attention for long and he soon moved to the more glamorous environs of Jurys Hotel on Dame Street.

Jurys Hotel belonged to one of Ireland's leading hotel-owning families. They were involved for many years in the Shelbourne in St Stephen's Green. When John Howard joined Jurys, the Shelbourne was managed by the dashing Captain Peter Jury. Jurys itself was managed by Bobby Kerr and later by Willie Opperman. The Copper Grill was the main restaurant in Jurys and it was strictly governed by head waiter, Joe Grey, of whom it was said no customer's name or face was ever forgotten. He later went on to open the Celtic Mews in Baggot Street, which still stands today as Derry Clarke's L'Ecrivain.

The Copper Grill enjoyed its greatest reputation under Swiss–German head chef Willy Widmer. He was one of the most formative influences on John Howard's early career. Working at Jurys gave the young Howard a formidable range of social contacts. The bar at Jurys was a fashionable meeting place in central Dublin. It was at Jurys that he met his future wife, Catherine Carroll, who came from Blackwater, County Wexford. They married in 1970 and their daughter Karen was born in 1973.

A need for broader experience rather than any sense of wanderlust took Howard away from Jurys and Dublin to London and Switzerland. He took up a job in L'Ecu de France in Jermyn Street. It was one of London's most fashionable restaurants and a favourite haunt of Princess Anne and her circle of Throne Rangers. The dining room had a domed ceiling and, therefore, an odd acoustic that lent itself perfectly to picking up snippets of Royal conversation by inquisitive souls at neighbouring tables. Le Caprice, the Mirabell, Wiltons and the old Quaglino's were just some of its main rivals.

On his days off, John visited many such establishments to sample his rivals' fare. It was also at this time that he began to build up his expert knowledge of wine. The Café Royal, made famous by another Irishman, Oscar Wilde, in an earlier time, was John Howard's next place of employment. It was here that he met chef, the late Dr Noel Cullen whose meticulous knowledge of food later led him to write the general syllabus for the training of chefs in the United States.

The Café Royal was followed by a brief spell – due to visa difficulties – in the Lausanne Palace Hotel in Switzerland. Founded in 1915 and commanding imposing views of the Alps, it was then one of the great hotels of the world and was patronised extensively by the wealthy Greek shipping community.

The year 1971 found John back in Ireland as head chef in Sutton House Hotel in Howth. Its owner, Paul Drumm, was married to the daughter of Albert Luykx who was one of the central cast of the Arms Trial. John Howard recalled that, on his return to Ireland, people seemed to speak of little other than the Arms Trial. He stayed at Sutton House for three years before moving for one season to the Courtown Hotel in Wexford. There would be one other move, to White's Hotel in Wexford, before returning to Dublin to open his own restaurant in 1977.

White's Hotel offered an excellent opportunity for the future chef-owner. The hotel traced its history to a hostelry called the King's Arms founded in 1700. It was a busy coaching inn throughout much of the nineteenth century and enjoyed a reputation for good food. Oscar Wilde's mother was born there in 1820, as was the Wexford Opera Festival in 1950.

By the time John Howard arrived in 1974, White's had added a new section to the hotel so that it could cater for the increasing demands made on the old establishment by events such as the Opera Festival. Wexford has long had a good reputation for quality food. The Lobster Pot at Carne, the Talbot, Kelly's in Rosslare and White's itself served a sophisticated clientele that included many of the patrons of the Wexford International Opera Festival. John Howard became friendly with opera goers, including Bernard Levin. On one occasion, for a festival production of *The Thief of Baghdad,* John produced a banquet centrepiece for the opera stage. It contained a suckling pig that was named "the pig of Baghdad". It was at this time that he started to gain the attention of the main food writers in Ireland and win the first of many national and international awards. Theodora FitzGibbon, writing in *The Irish Times,* hailed his efforts at White's as "producing among the best food in Ireland".

With such praise for his cooking by then becoming a regular thing, John and Catherine decided to take the daunting step of leaving the security of White's to open their own restaurant. Dublin, which they both knew well, was their preferred location. They made the move to the capital with their young daughter Karen. The year was 1977.

2 *"I Present John Howard Cooking"*

'… You do honour to bring a guest here.'

Terry O'Sullivan
On his first visit to *Le Coq Hardi*
Dubliner's Diary, March 1977

Left: Catherine Howard
Below: John Howard

*J*ohn and Catherine Howard opened *Le Coq Hardi* in March 1977 in the basement of the Landsdowne Hotel at 29 Pembroke Road. The monthly rent was £75. Within weeks of its opening, a review by Jim Dunne in *Business and Finance* hailed it as "one of the top three restaurants in the capital". In the December 1977 issue of *Magill* magazine, *Le Coq Hardi* advertised lunch at just under £3 and dinner for £7.

Reigning supreme over Dublin's restaurant proprietor-chefs at that time was the rather grand and ample figure of Seán Kinsella. His Mirabeau was the *sine qua non* for all that aspired to, or had already acquired, the better things of life in Dublin. A restaurant listing at the time warned that "you can get by on £10 per head at the Mirabeau, but if you have to worry about the prices, don't go there".

Kinsella was famous for throwing Peter-Langan-style tantrums in the restaurant. Bills were ritually torn up if a customer complained and they were told never to darken his famous door again. It was all a great floorshow. There are many that hailed and some that still hail Kinsella as one of the greatest chefs Ireland ever produced. Prices did not appear on his menus. Some patrons felt that the bills were arrived at by some form of secret sorcery.

Kinsella himself was a flamboyant character ideally suited to running such a colourful establishment. He drove about Dublin in a Rolls Royce and wore the finest bespoke suits. Unlike many chefs in Dublin and elsewhere, Kinsella was not a drinker. His antics in the restaurant are the stuff of legend.

In contrast, there were no public tantrums thrown by the owner-chef at *Le Coq Hardi*. The restaurant was named after two establishments of the same name in London and Lyons. John selected, as his first location, a basement premises in Pembroke Road. Situated between fashionable Ballsbridge and St Stephen's Green, the road was a perfect catchment area from which to entice the clientele from nearby hotels and offices. The Lansdowne Hotel was overhead and several good public houses were nearby. "The Pirates' Den" was the pub attached to the restaurant premises. The showgrounds of the Royal Dublin Society were just down the road and the United States embassy added further to the prestigious location. Its proximity to some of Dublin's nightclubs also did it no harm. The dubious delights of Leeson Street Liebefraumilch, of Barbarella's and Zhivago's – where, according to its ads, love stories began – were all just a biscuit's throw from Pembroke Road.

There were eleven tables that catered for forty covers. The general look was of chipped and faded elegance and a green curtain just about shielded the chef from his more curious patrons. Despite limited resources, a high standard of decoration was aimed at. Good china, linen and glassware were sourced locally. "Like all top class restaurants," opined that galloping gourmet Terry O'Sullivan in his *Evening Press* diary, "*Le Coq Hardi* is intimate, softly lit, gleaming and murmuring. You do honour to bring a guest here" was his final exhortation to his readers. He did warn them that the restaurant did not, on opening, have a telephone but the Lansdowne Hotel upstairs took reservations, while the nice men from Post and Telegraphs looked for a spare phone line. It was not unusual to wait three years for a telephone line at that time.

The gossip press soon started to carry the news of this new establishment. "A bird like an undernourished mini-chicken for £12!" ran one headline shocker. It referred to that most noble and delicious of birds, the grouse, whose own social diary becomes rather hectic after 12 August (or 1 September in Ireland) when the grouse season starts. "The grouse have nothing to fear from the people who shoot them" the Duke of Edinburgh, using his own sublime logic, once remarked.

John Howard shot his own grouse on occasion or purchased them from Tommy Mulloy of Baggot Street, the last of the gentlemen fishmongers in Dublin, in whose shop not only good game and fish can still be found but also excellent conversation. John insisted on young grouse. He sealed them on the pan before roasting for no more than thirty minutes, so that they were just pink on the bone when they landed on the table. They were served with game chips, and game gravy made from the roasting juices. He thinks bread sauce is one of the most redundant things to appear on any table. (See his recipe for Roast Grouse on page 52.) For its first grouse season, *Le Coq Hardi* had just three birds for sale. It required the selling of two at £12 each to cover the cost of the birds. To put that in another perspective, the average rent for a flat in Dublin in 1977 was about £15 a week, a beer in a night club was around 50 pence a pint, a gin and tonic 65 pence and a bottle of something vaguely resembling wine was £4.95. Oh, the days of the Kerry dancers!

The week it opened, *Le Coq Hardi* offered lunch for three, with a bottle of wine for the remarkably good value of £16.25. John Howard told the press

Front entrance of Le Coq Hardi

that his intention was to have a French restaurant. That did not mean gingham tablecloths, excessive use of garlic and cream and stratospheric prices. He told journalists he belonged to the classic school of French cooking. To others, he would say "there is no alchemy involved". Though an admirer of many great French chefs, he developed his own individual style: "I present John Howard cooking" he would exclaim to anyone who asked about his influences. He admires Escoffier, Carême, Jacques Maximin and others, but he made his own golden rules from the day he opened on Pembroke Road.

The chief of these was never serve food that is out of season. "Pacific oysters have given oysters a bad name because they do not have a season," he would say. From his first day in business, he insisted on supervising the purchase of his vegetables at market early each morning. Vegetables were caressed, sniffed, eyeballed and measured before they passed his exacting standards. Even the presence of the occasional hangover would not keep the chef-proprietor away from the very early morning fruit and vegetable market. As many as ten different vegetables might be used on an average day at *Le Coq Hardi*.

The initial reviews were all that a newly established restaurant could hope for. Perhaps the most important came from that great doyenne of Irish food criticism, Theodora FitzGibbon. She exerted a powerful sway over opinion on such matters. Her views became the set opinions of many middle-class matrons of Dublin. In later years, John often contacted her if unsure about the history of a certain dish. She had Mrs Beaton-like knowledge of English cooking. Writing in her column in *The Irish Times,* she described John Howard's food as "impeccable".

Within a very short time of opening its doors, the restaurant had gathered a loyal following. In a time when entertaining in restaurants was allowable against tax, John Howard's main problem was getting the lunchtime guests out before the dinner guests arrived. This was not the era of the "one glass" luncheon or the "no glass" luncheon. It was not unusual for lunchtime patrons to have a few gin and tonics, white wine, red wine and finish off with port or brandy before heading back to the office. The public relations companies became big supporters, as was Bill Ambrose of *Business and Finance* and Vincent Daly, MD of Ericsson. Jim Dunne loved the place so much that quarter of a century later he still kept as a souvenir his first receipt from the restaurant.

No great establishment could function without loyal and dedicated staff. The first chef to work alongside John Howard in the kitchen of the restaurant was Noel Kenny. Front of house alongside Catherine was headwaiter, Philip Duggan, who had worked with John in L'Ecu de France. With him was Patrick Martin, now Ireland's Honorary Consul in Bermuda and John Gordon, a young Scottish waiter. Jimmy O'Sullivan joined John as chef in the kitchen and twenty-one years later, he was still with *Le Coq Hardi*. The best-known name, however, to work beside John was award-winning chef Derry Clarke, whose own l'Ecrivain is now one of the most celebrated restaurants in Ireland.

For two and a half years, the restaurant remained in its basement location. Business went from strength to strength and *Le Coq Hardi* began to develop a reputation not just at home but also abroad. Reviews began appearing in UK and American publications. With this growing success came the pressure to find a new location for the restaurant. The Howards were firmly of the view that the prosperous Ballsbridge area was where their continued success would be assured. Just a few doors up from their restaurant, they spotted the slightly down-at-heel building that contained The Embassy Hotel. It had an ideal corner location fronting Pembroke Road and running along the side of the fashionable Wellington Road. A flight of imposing granite steps led up to the hall door. A stone eagle stood sentinel over the doorcase. The two-bay house had a cream-painted façade, and a wide forecourt allowed ample parking. A railing protected the building from the busy street.

When the Howards enquired, they found that the building was for sale. It had belonged to a retired Canadian pilot, Vincent Glover, and was offered for sale by his heirs for £150,000. With the finances at *Le Coq Hardi* looking healthy, the Howards decided to approach their bankers for a loan. John telephoned Allied Irish bank, who immediately offered him one hundred per cent finance for the building at a staggering interest rate of twenty-two per cent. In these days of low-interest rates such a figure seems scarcely credible, but with a pressing need to expand, the deal was signed and work commenced on the new restaurant almost immediately.

The building was badly run down. Architects Diamond, Redfern, Anderson were engaged to design the new *Coq Hardi*. They had done, amongst others, Lock's Restaurant on the canal and Inigo Jones in London. The Howards sought

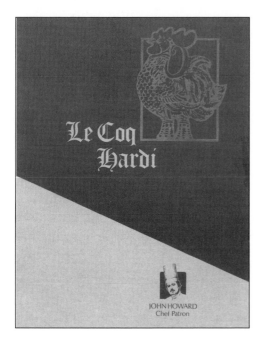

<table>
</table>

Le Coq Hardi
RESTAURANT
Tel : 01/689070
29 Pembroke Road, Ballsbridge, Dublin 4.
Chef Patron: **JOHN HOWARD**   Date: 19/1/ 19 80.

For Table 11.

	£	p
2 Soup.	1.	80.
2 Garlic steak	12.	85.
Vegetable.	2.	20.
1 Dessert.	1.	50
2 Coffee.	1.	00
	19.	35
12½% Service.	2.	40
	21.	75
Discount.	5.	44
a little thought of 21 years ago	16.	31
TOTAL		

Le Coq Hardi

35 Pembroke Road, Dublin 4. Tel: 698070

"John Howard, Dublin's most talented chef, specializes in French cooking".

(Essen & Trinken: 'Dublin-Tips'.)

Le Coq Hardi

JOHN HOWARD
Chef Patron

Above: John's fame spreads to Germany
Above left: An early bill
Below left: The first menu cover

Above: Catherine at home

Above left: John, Karen and Catherine Howard

Left: (left to right) Gearóid Lynch, John, Glen Clifford and Jimmy O'Sullivan

the solid look of a gentleman's club coupled with all the amenities needed to operate a thoroughly modern kitchen. Denis Anderson led the team. The look was later completed by designer Peter Johnson, who placed on *Le Coq Hardi* that sophisticated glamorous stamp that most of its patrons will remember.

A welcoming long, wide entrance hall set the tone. Large-domed silver carving trolleys lurked with welcoming intent. The walls were hung with many of the parchment testaments to the culinary prowess of the chef-patron. Pictures of his successful horses also represented John's interest in horse racing. Turning the corner, a mahogany glass-fronted bookcase contained a veritable regiment of vintage Armagnac, Cognac and whiskey, all lined up by age and rank and standing proudly to attention as honour guard to the passing guest. Downstairs an elegant bar served as an anteroom. It had an inviting open fire and copies of the famous tables designed by Sam Stephenson in 1957 for the Horseshoe Bar at the Shelbourne Hotel.

The dining room divided easily and practically by its original room structure into two parts and formed an L-shape. At the back, to the left as one entered, the kitchen was visible to all through a generous service hatch. One wall was wood-panelled and hung with three vast mirrors, which reflected light from around the room. The two front windows were hung with heavy drapes. Bergère dining chairs, crisp linen, glassware and the *Coq Hardi* signature dinner plates and a good collection of Irish paintings helped form a welcoming ambience. Fresh flowers were always noticeable. The overall feeling was of clubby comfort. On the mantelpiece, bottles of red wine chosen by John Howard to match the day's menu stood anxiously awaiting the eye of the curious diner.

The restaurant catered for forty-five covers, and regulars frequently did battle for their favourite tables. One such customer, who prefers anonymity, has his own theory on this phenomenon. He says that "in any restaurant, there are only three tables of consequence. This positioning is formulaic and a matter of precise mathematical calculation. Recognising them comes naturally to the seasoned diner who knows instinctively that the others are for tourists!" He also insists that if in doubt on the often-vexed matter of placement, one should resort to the methods of Catherine the Great. It was her habit to insist that guests, irrespective of rank or sex, would draw lots for a place at table. Over such heady matters have kingdoms

Above: Garden-level bar
Left: Entrance hall
Below: The main dining room

been lost! Whilst the battle for the key tables ensued upstairs, menus could be consulted over a drink in the intimate downstairs or, more correctly, garden-level bar. The first floor housed the inner sanctum of the private dining room that is described elsewhere in this book. Many of the old patrons and several new ones made their way to the new premises of *Le Coq Hardi*.

In essence, John's cooking remained loyal to his old formula. "There is nothing new about cooking" he has said in numerous interviews. He has always readily acknowledged the paramount influence of France on his craft. He points out that such tradition as there was in Irish cooking was essentially dominated by the owners of the great Irish country houses and their chefs and cooks. The Earl of Kingston's chef at Mitchelstown Castle in County Cork was a man called Claridge who went on to open the famous hotel bearing his name in London. The *métier* of these Big House kitchens was essentially French-influenced English cooking.

With the establishment of the Free State and the demise of the Big House much of that tradition died out. "Tradition in Irish cooking as we now know it," John Howard says "dates only from the late sixties, when Ireland began to emerge from a period of austerity. Then the nursemaids of our fledgling food culture were a handful of French chefs working in our leading hotels." He recalled that when he started out in the food business "everywhere from Bushmills to Ballybunion, there were chefs murdering excellent Irish ingredients. By and large chefs were not making the most of the excellent raw materials – lamb, salmon, oysters, pork, and, particularly, the vegetables which they were cooking to a mush". His one regret about the business in Ireland is the failure of Irish vegetables, unlike our meats and cheeses, to realise their potential. He does admit that things have come a long way from the days when one bought a bag of potatoes consisting of eight different sizes and at the bottom sat a load of stones!

Even in the early 1980s, chefs who required supplies of food that were in any way out of the ordinary often found themselves faced with difficulties. "One of my problems," John Howard recalls, "was to find a reliable and continual source of high-quality seasonal, fresh and occasionally exotic ingredients. Many promised this service but in my experience only Pallas Food have provided and maintained the standards of the great French purveyors. We are lucky to have this level of dedication to product in Ireland." In 1986 chef Patrick Clement arrived in Dublin from France. That year he entered a competition for which he wished to prepare Magret of Duck. He was unable to find the duck he required for the dish in Ireland and his sister had to bring it over from Paris in time for the competition. The finest magret come from ducks boned the day after they are killed, and are served the day after that.

Patrick now works with Pallas Foods based in Newcastle West, County Limerick. The Geary family founded the company in the year Patrick arrived in Dublin. He says his life as a chef here would have been made considerably easier, if the 2,500 products Pallas now supplies had been available to him then. Pallas Foods provides the food industry with food products sourced in Ireland, whenever possible, but also sourced in Italy, France, Belgium, Spain, the US, Switzerland, Holland and all over Asia. He says the exotic nature of some of the products supplied by Pallas is an indicator of how tastes have changed in Ireland. "We have been asked to supply ostrich and crocodile as well as prime Irish beef," he says. "Today people understand the difference between black and white truffles in the way they would previously have understood the difference between black and white pudding and it is wonderful that we are asked to provide both!"

Patrick Clement says that John Howard played a major role in advancing the appreciation of good food in Ireland. He is proud that the company, when asked to find grouse for a dinner in John's honour, was able to source it in Wicklow and not in Scotland, the bird's more traditional habitat. Grouse, as we have seen earlier, was one of the first game dishes served in the early days of *Le Coq Hardi*. John welcomes the fact that chefs can now rely on Irish food companies, like his old friends at Pallas, to provide them with not just the exotic but with a guaranteed range of top-quality Irish products.

John recalls that for anyone learning the business around the time he started, "it was *de rigueur* to get the plane to Paris or the boat to Holyhead". Many of them did not return but John Howard was happy to do so and in the process, put his own stamp on the development of Irish cooking. He gives credit to other pioneers in the field such as Patrick Guilbaud, the Ryans at Arbutus Lodge, Gerry Galvin at the Vintage in Kinsale, the Allens at Ballymaloe, the O'Callaghans at Longueville, the Bowe family at Marlfield, and Aidan MacManus

Nicholas Allas, Michael Birch, Catherine, Darren Campbell and José Martinhoe

Above: Birthday celebrations at the Wexford Opera Festival with Lord Moyne and Dr A.H. Hughes

Below: John with Paul Bocuse
Below left: An early review

John and Catherine Howard — Le Coq Hardi, 29 Pembroke Road, Dublin 4.

"Nearly all restauranteurs come from Clare".

News to me! John does, so does Sean Kinsella and there are many others in the city. John reached Le Coq Hardi via Lausanne and London. These are more formal cities than ours, perhaps that is why he feels strongly about being correctly dressed. He wouldn't dream of going out for dinner without a jacket and tie. Dining out is an occasion, being correctly dressed shows a sense of respect for the restaurant and the other diners.

Smoking between courses "shows a total lack of appreciation for the food and wine, how could anyone savour a sauce after ten or fifteen cigarettes?"

John is open to criticism provided it's justified, if it isn't, he believes in getting his point across "stick to your own thinking, customers shouldn't run your business for you." Often a customer finds fault with a dish because they don't like what they have ordered or they have ordered an ill balanced meal but most often because they are having a quarrel! John has a large

following of 'regulars', people he would telephone if he had a special dish on. He loves to cook for those who appreciate it, like all of us he is delighted when his efforts are praised, compliments come more readily from foreigners than from the Irish.

John's wife Catherine works with him, when they are free they like to eat out. Where? In Dublin he feels the "Berkeley Court" looks after him well, outside Dublin the "Arbutus Lodge" in Cork, they both agree that it deserves all its accolades. John generously says of the owner Declan Ryan, "I think he's one of the finest chefs in Europe." What is his favourite dish? Fish, "one of our greatest raw materials" but never from a fish farm.

What would be his ambition? This he is very close to achieving. In a short while he shall be moving to his new premises two doors away, (35, Pembroke Street). "It will be more elegant with a super interesting wine cellar. I shall even have my own herb garden, in fact I think it's the best location in Dublin".

continued on page 70

at the King Sitric. Nor is he slow to give due credit to the new generation of chefs like Michael Clifford, Derry Clarke, the Rankins, Robbie Millar and Kevin Thornton and Dan Mullane.

Throughout its quarter of a century in existence, *Le Coq Hardi* offered the classical French cooking in which John Howard was trained and in which he placed his absolute trust. The appellation French-Irish was often given to his cooking style but that annoyed him. As trends changed so too did elements of John's cooking methods. His cooking was not stuck in a time warp. His sauces were modified to make them lighter. New and more interesting ingredients were always in evidence. Fads and trends were ignored. His aim was to create a restaurant of honest food with the best Irish raw materials. Part of his genius was to make the so-called "ordinary" seem special. Under his classically trained French hand, black and white pudding, shank of lamb, silverside, liver, rabbit and even the humble cabbage acquired a sophistication all of their own.

It was this uncompromising belief in the superiority of the French classical style that brought *Le Coq Hardi* to the very forefront of the league of great restaurants in Europe. Such success is never without its trials and tribulations and, certainly, involved a very great deal of hard work. When *Le Coq Hardi* was at its prime, it was not unusual for John and Catherine to put in an eighteen-hour day.

The new establishment also had its loyal and dedicated staff. *Le Coq Hardi* had, on average, twelve staff members between kitchen and front of house. Jimmy O'Sullivan was joined in the kitchen by new chefs that included Gearóid Lynch from Cavan and Paul Doyle who worked with the Roux brothers and at the Dorchester. Patrons will remember the large and varied cast that comprised the front of house team over the years. They included Catherine's sister Mary Carroll who knew all the regular customers and managed the office; Bruno Bertha who also worked with Patrick Guilbaud and now owns Bruno's in Kildare Street; Pat Garth and Pat Boyle; Nicholas Allas who also worked at Guilbaud's and stayed at *Le Coq Hardi* for twelve years; Michael Birch and José Martinhoe were also there for twelve years and immensely popular with the customers; and Darren Campbell from Dublin was on staff for five years. One vital behind-the-scenes figure was housekeeper Maureen Murphy from Ballyfermot. She arrived by bicycle

at seven o'clock each morning and began her task of tackling the vast amount of linen from the previous day's dining.

Throughout its happy history, *Le Coq Hardi* witnessed many extraordinary events. It was used to mark moments in political history, business deals were sealed and engagements, marriages and divorces too had their moments there. Celebrities both native and foreign pitched up there. Two glamorous prostitutes took their clothes off when their gentlemen were once refused last drinks late at night. Hundreds of loyal customers came back repeatedly to enjoy the unique experience it offered. To mention any here would run the risk of leaving out some trusted and loyal customer and invoke the wrath of others. They know that John and Catherine cherished their loyal following. The Howards knew that no matter how fine the restaurant they had, it would have been of little use to them without the patrons who returned again and again to the sign of *Le Coq Hardi* at Pembroke Road. Looking back at many of the old menus on John's file, what strikes one is that the restaurant offered extraordinarily good value for such superb food and service.

In 1995, the legend very nearly came to a premature end in the most tragic fashion. On the morning of 15 December, a fire was discovered on the garden level of the building in the laundry room next to the main cellar. Catherine heard the news on the car radio. Her daughter Karen who rushed to the scene was advised to stay back by the fire officers present, but dashed in to save her father's humidor containing his cigar collection. Extensive damage was caused to the building and over £50,000 worth of fine wines was lost from the cellar. They included some of the 1920s and 1930s Mouton, 1963 Port, some Yquem and a selection of vintage Armagnac.

Undaunted by the task facing them, the Howards set about a new scheme of decoration and restoration and within months, they were open again for business. John went searching wine collections to replace his lost treasures. Patrons flocked back to wish them well. A whole new ambience was created and business continued to prosper.

In later years, John had a little more time to enjoy other pursuits. He has always enjoyed two other great passions apart from the food business – the Turf and collecting paintings and antiques. Figures from the racing world such as Dermot Weld, Jim Bolger, Noel Meade, Bert Firestone, John Magnier, Paul Carbery, Michael Kinnane, J.P. McManus and many others were regulars at *Le Coq Hardi*. Photographs of John's own winners hung in the entrance hall. His first horse was Ballyvaughan Boy, trained by Noel Meade, and the winner of seven races. Others followed including Corkscrew Hill, Burren Symphony, Another Coq Hardi, Dublin's Coq Hardi, Coq Hardi Diamond and the great Coq Hardi Affair, which won or was placed in sixteen races for John, before being killed in the Irish Grand National in 1995. At the same meeting the jockey, Shane Broderick, broke his back and John and Catherine organised a benefit dinner for him in the restaurant.

When not engaged in the restaurant or on the Turf, John pursued his passion for collecting Irish artists and antiques. He has one of the largest col-

Ballyvaughan Boy

John, Pat Leech and Noel Meade

The Horse Fair at Oughterard by Kenneth Webb

A Study of A Horse by Walter Osborne

*Oil painting of Coq Hardi Affair
by John King*

Coq Hardi Affair ridden by Paul Carberry

lections of antique oil lamps in the world and it compliments his collection of Irish furniture and paintings.

The decision to close was not an easy one and was made only after the deepest reflection and with considerable regret. John felt that EU bureaucracy had contributed greatly to hampering small family businesses such as his. By then that seemed somewhat irrelevant, given his achievements. John had been at the helm of his own restaurant for over quarter of a century. He had been cooking since his teenage years and, by the time he made his decision to retire, he was a legend in the culinary world at home and abroad. He had been honoured by a lifetime achievement award by his peers in the industry in Ireland. His food had graced some of the most famous tables around the world, including the White House and the Waldorf Astoria. He had catered for presidents, princes and captains of industry from Dublin to Monte Carlo; the latter where he had catered for one of Dr Michael Smurfit's most glamorous parties. He counted among his friends some of the great chefs of the world, including Paul Bocuse.

Whenever his name is mentioned, it is always with great affection and there are many that wish he were still in business. *Le Coq Hardi* closed its doors to its last customer on 30 March 2001. The building was bought first by John Foley and later resold and became the headquarters of Morgans Wines. For the many thousands who passed through its doors, *Le Coq Hardi* remains a special memory of a great Irish institution.

3 *John Howard Recipes*

Coq Hardi Smokies

Ingredients

Tomato concasse (Recipe below)
400 g undyed smoked haddock
200 g Gruyère cheese, finely grated
Finely chopped coriander or parsley

Freshly ground pepper, to taste
Lemon
Brown bread
30 ml cream

Tomato Concasse

- Plunge 6 large ripe tomatoes into boiling water – then straight into iced cold water. Remove the skin – cut in half and remove the seeds. Chop the tomato flesh finely. Sauté finely chopped shallot and garlic for a few minutes, then add tomatoes and a dash of white wine. Simmer for 15 minutes.

Method

- Remove the skin and pin bones from the smoked haddock and chop into small cubes.

- Into 4 Ramekin dishes, place half the tomato concasse, fill with smoked haddock, almost to the top, add remaining tomato, coriander or parsley, pepper and cream. Top with grated cheese.

- Bake in oven Gas Mark 8, 220°C (425°F) for 20–25 minutes.

To Serve

- Serve with lemon and brown bread.

Serves: 4

Soup a l'Oignon Gratineé

Ingredients

12 onions (medium sized)
4 tablespoons oil plus butter, mixed
1.25 l good beef stock
½ clove garlic, crushed
½ glass cognac or champagne
Freshly ground black pepper and salt, to taste
1 French bread, cut in rounds and toasted
Grated Gruyère cheese

Method

- Peel and slice onions, heat oil and butter in a large saucepan; add the onions and cook gently until golden brown. Add the beef stock gradually, stirring constantly until the soup boils. Add the crushed garlic plus black pepper and salt. Simmer slowly for 40 minutes; add cognac or champagne. (The addition of garlic and Cognac is not asked for in the traditional French country recipe.)

- Half-fill oven-proof earthenware soup bowls with the rounds of French bread, fill the bowls with onion soup; sprinkle with plenty of grated Gruyère cheese and bake in a fairly hot oven until golden brown and bubbling.

Serves: 6

Black and White Pudding with Apple and Raisin Compote

Ingredients

8 slices black and white pudding
3 knobs of butter
4 tablespoons mashed potato
1 tablespoon onion, very finely chopped
1 tablespoon ham, very finely chopped
1 tablespoon parsley, very finely chopped
Salt and black pepper, to taste
2 apples, diced and cooked in a little water, sugar and lemon juice
1 tablespoon raisins
3 tablespoons beef stock
Dash of Irish whiskey

Method

@→ Cook the black and white pudding gently in hot butter, set aside. Mix the potato, onion, ham, parsley and seasoning together. Shape into 8 little cakes. Cook, also in hot butter, until well browned. Stir the raisins into the cooked apple. Heat the beef stock, flavour lightly with whiskey, add a knob of butter and season to taste.

To Serve

@→ Place the potato cakes and black and white pudding slices on each plate. Spoon on the apple and raisin compote. Finish with a little of the sauce.

Serves: 4

Soufflé d' Homard

Ingredients

9 egg yolks
10 tablespoons dry Vermouth
Salt and pepper, to taste
6 soup spoons whipped cream
2 x 600 g cooked lobsters
20 ml glacé américaine *sauce, reduced*
Cayenne pepper, to taste
Lemon juice
12 egg whites
80 g butter
20 g flour

Method

- Make a sabayon by whipping egg yolks and Vermouth over boiling water until it thickens. Season with salt and pepper, add cream. Slice lobster tails and claws. Keep 12 nice slices aside and make a ragout (salpicon) with the rest mixed with the *glacé américaine*. Season with salt, pepper, cayenne pepper, and a drop of lemon juice. Whip eggwhites with a pinch of salt but not too stiffly. Butter and flour 6 soufflé dishes.

- Mix the lobster ragout with the sabayon and gradually add the egg whites. Place mixture into dishes and bake for 5 minutes in the oven at Gas Mark 4, 180°C (350°F). Remove from oven and place 2 slices of remaining lobster on top of each soufflé. Bake again for 8 minutes. Serve immediately.

Serves: 6

Terrine of Clonakilty Black & White Pudding ... with Compôte of Apple and Poached Egg

Ingredients

½ ring of black pudding
½ ring of white pudding
8 rindless back rashers
250 g puréed chicken breast
Freshly ground black pepper, to taste
2 cooking apples, peeled and chopped
25 g sugar
25 g butter
8 eggs
2 teaspoons white wine vinegar

Method

- Skin the black and white pudding and put each in a small bowl. Divide the chicken between two bowls and mix well. Season with black pepper.

- Line a small terrine mould with the rashers. Fill firstly with black pudding and smooth with a palate knife. Then add the white pudding and fold over the bacon, cover with tin foil and bake in a moderate oven, in a *bain-marie* of water for 30 minutes. Remove from oven to allow to cool – overnight, if possible.

Apple Compôte

- Put apple, sugar and butter in a pot with a little water and cook. Do not make sauce too smooth. You may add a teaspoon of calvados if you wish.

- Poach eggs in boiling water with some vinegar – leaves the egg soft.

To Serve

- Slice the terrine into slices about 1 inch thick and fry in some melted butter for a couple of minutes on either side. Serve surrounded by the apple compôte and a poached egg on top.

Serves: 8

Andouillette de Saumon en Habit Vert

Ingredients

3 tablespoons finely
   chopped shallots
Butter, as needed
50 ml plus
   ½ bottle dry white wine
Sea salt and freshly ground
   black pepper, to taste
375 ml thick cream
50 ml chicken stock
200 g blanched watercress

1 tablespoon chopped chives
100 ml water
1 tablespoon lemon juice
200 g salmon fillet
2 egg whites
4 x 100 g fillets of salmon
Blanched spinach leaves, as needed
Fish stock, as needed
Watercress, to garnish

Crème de Cresson Sauce

Sweat 2/3 shallots of butter until translucent. Add 50 ml of wine, salt and milled pepper and boil until reduced to 2 tablepoons of purée. Boil two-thirds of cream with the chicken stock until reduced by two-thirds. Let cool. When cold, put into a liquidiser with blanched watercress, chives, water and lemon juice. Check seasoning and store, covered, in refrigerator until required.

Method

Pass the 200 g of salmon fillet through a food processor with egg whites, salt, and black pepper for 1 minute. Add remaining cream and run for 30 seconds. Allow to rest in refrigerator for 1 hour.

> Gently flatten the 4 salmon fillets into a rectangle by placing them between 2 sheets of cling film and gently tapping with a smooth meat hammer. Place onto a single layer of overlapping spinach leaves.

> Season the salmon and spread a $1/8$ inch layer of mousse on the salmon. Roll up like a Swiss roll. Butter a heavy ovenproof dish and place the salmon on the bottom, sprinkle with remaining shallots, add $1/2$ bottle white wine and enough fish stock to cover the sides of the salmon by one-third.

> Cover and cook for 15 minutes in an oven at Gas Mark 5, 190°C (375°F). Drain and keep warm between 2 plates. Reduce the cooking juices by one-third, add the prepared crème de cresson sauce, and boil to a thick but pouring consistency.

To Serve

> Pour sauce onto warm plates and dress salmon on top with a small sprig of watercress.

Serves: 4

Shin of Beef Terrine, with a Horseradish Dressing & Gherkins

Ingredients

1.5 kg shin of beef trimmed
2 medium leeks
1 clove garlic
150 g onions
100 g celeriac
100 g carrots
Chopped chives
Thyme, bay leaf, parsley and peppercorns
Salt
2–2½ litres water

Method

- Put shin into cold water, bring to the boil, remove and refresh in cold water. Trim any gristle and fat.

- Place beef in a heavy-bottom saucepan, cover with water, bring to the boil and simmer.

- Add the herbs and peppercorns, cook for 2½ to 3 hours, until almost cooked. Add the vegetables and garlic.

- Remove the vegetables when they are cooked – cool them and chop into a fine dice. Separate the leeks into leaves.

Line a terrine with the leeks, allowing them to overlap the edges. Place a layer of the beef, which you should have roughly flaked, in the bottom. Press down, add a layer of vegetables and chives, then another layer of meat. Repeat the process until you have three layers of meat and two layers of vegetables.

Meanwhile, strain the stock – allow it to settle – you may need to add some gelatine. It should be gelatinous when cool. Pour this stock into the mould and cover meat completely. Chill overnight until set.

To Serve

Arrange a slice of terrine on a plate, garnish with some dressed salad leaves, serve with a light horseradish sauce or dressing and some finely sliced gherkins.

Serves: 5

White Lamb Stew with Baby Vegetables & Sorrel

Ingredients

1.7 kg shoulder lamb
4 carrots, cut in nice shapes
3 bay leaves
Whole black peppercorns
2 bunches of sorrel, cut in large pieces
Salt and pepper
2 litres good lamb
    or chicken stock
1 kg pearl onions

4 cloves garlic, crushed
100 grams wild mushrooms,
    roughly cut
500 ml. white wine
10 baby white turnips, peeled and
    leave some of green top on
Some lightly whipped cream
    (about 3 tablespoons)

Method

- Cut the meat into cubes, remove any fat, bring to boil and refresh in cold water.

- Place the lamb, with carrots, onions, turnips, garlic, bay leaves, peppercorns and wild mushrooms into a thick-bottom saucepan, pour over white wine and stock.

- Bring to the boil and simmer gently for $1\frac{1}{2}$ hours or until meat is tender, but do not overcook or the meat will be dry.

- When cooked, strain meat and vegetables and return stock to reduce, thicken very slightly. Add a few spoons of lightly whipped cream, season with salt and pepper. Return the meat and vegetables to sauce, add sorrel. Heat carefully, serve with new potatoes.

Serves: 5

Roast Fillet of Hake with Tomato and Black Olives

Ingredients

2 kg hake fillet, with skin on,
  cut into 4 pieces
400 g new potatoes
20 g crushed garlic
50 ml good virgin olive oil
30 g chopped dill or chervil
Salt and pepper
100 g black olives

Method

- Steam the new potatoes in their skins. When cooked and still warm, peel and crush with a fork. Add warm olive oil to enrich the potatoes and season with salt, pepper, garlic and chopped herbs. Keep warm.

Sauce

- Warm olive oil with chopped olives and season with salt, pepper and lemon juice. Add chopped herbs and diced tomato. Cook the hake in virgin olive oil, ensuring the skin side is very crispy.

To Serve

- Place a large tablespoon of the potato in the centre of plates. Spoon the sauce around the potato. Place the fish on top and serve immediately, very hot.

Serves: 8

Coq au Vin — Coq Hardi

Ingredients

1 large chicken,
    jointed into 8 pieces
250 g streaky bacon
250 g tiny shallots
2 teaspoons Cognac
1 bottle red Burgundy
1 cup veal stock
2 whole cloves garlic

1 bouquet garni,
    sprig of thyme, bay-leaf and parsley
    tied together in a muslin bag
500 g mixed mushrooms
4 tablespoons butter
Beurre manié
Salt and black pepper

Method

- Cut the bacon into lardons and blanch. Fry the pieces in butter in a heavy casserole dish. Sauté the chicken and the onions until they are lightly coloured. Warm the Cognac and flame the bird. Add wine, stock, garlic and bouquet garni, then bring to a simmer. Cover the casserole and cook very slowly until the chicken is tender and cooked through.

- Remove the garlic cloves and the bouquet garni and add the shallots. Cook the mushrooms in butter and slip them into the casserole dish. Add enough small pieces of *beurre manié* (equal quantities of butter and flour) to thicken the sauce to a rich, creamy consistency. Cook gently for another ten minutes and adjust the seasoning before serving.

I also like to do this dish with a puff pastry lid as an interesting variation.

Serves: 4

Roast Grouse

Ingredients

4 young grouse, with livers if available
1 red apple, cored
1 orange
1 small onion, chopped
Salt
Freshly ground black pepper
75 ml olive oil
8 thin slices of pork fat or unsmoked bacon
60 g butter
4 slices of bread with crusts removed
60 ml melted butter
Watercress
Game chips (crisps)
Dash of Cognac

Method

- Heat oven to Gas Mark 8, 220°C (425°F). Wipe the birds carefully, inside and out with a damp cloth.

- Chop the apple, the orange and the zest of the orange, put them in a bowl, add the onion, salt and pepper and moisten with 15 ml of olive oil.

- Pack the grouse cavities tightly with the mixture, seal the cavity with a needle and thread.

- Rub the birds with black pepper, bard the breast of each with two slices of pork fat or bacon and tie into place.

- Place the birds in a roasting tin and put 15 g of butter on top.

- Roast the grouse for 35 minutes. Ten minutes before the end of cooking, remove the barding fat in order to allow the birds to brown.

- Meanwhile, before the grouse are ready, fry the slices of bread in olive oil and melted butter until golden brown. Drain on absorbent paper and keep warm.

- In a small pan sauté the grouse livers in a little butter, add a dash of Cognac and season with salt and pepper.

- Discard the orange and apple mixture.

To Serve

- Spread the croûtons with the liver mixture and place a grouse on each croûton. Garnish with watercress and serve with game chips.

- It is also traditional to serve a bread sauce or game gravy with grouse.

  Serves: 4

Roast Smoked Loin of Pork with Herb Mash, Buttered Cabbage and Cider Jus

This is an awarding-winning pork dish from John Howard

Ingredients

1½ kg smoked loin of pork (Kassler)
250 ml cider
Sprig of thyme
1 kg creamy mashed potatoes,
    kept warm
2 tablespoons chives and parsley

4–6 tablespoons very finely chopped
    cabbage, cooked in a small
    amount of water, salt and butter
8–12 roast shallots
Butter

Method

- Set oven to Gas Mark 6, 200°C (400°F). Roast the Kassler for approx ½–1 hour.

- Halfway through cooking, add in the cider and thyme. When the meat is cooked, wrap and keep warm. Boil up the juices in the pan. Set aside. Mix the creamy potatoes with the chives and parsley.

To Serve

- Pipe or spoon the potatoes onto the plate. Carve the meat and lay on the bed of potato. Spoon cabbage onto the plate plus the roast shallots. Finally, boil up the juices again with a knob of butter. Taste for seasoning and spoon around the meat.

Serves: 4

Braised Beef in Guinness

This is my variation of Boef Bourguignonne.

Ingredients

1 kg shoulder beef, cut into thin slices
2 tablespoon olive oil
1 onion, chopped
2 leeks, 2 carrots, 2 celery sticks, chopped
2 cloves garlic
250 ml well-reduced beef stock
125 ml Guinness
Salt and pepper
50 g butter
75 g streaky bacon, diced
100 g wild mushrooms, if available, sliced
50 g small onions, peeled
25 g flour

Method

- Heat the oil in a large pan, brown the meat well. Remove to a pot. Next, sauté the leeks, carrots and celery. Add to the meat plus the garlic. Pour in the stock and Guinness, season. Simmer gently for approx. 1½ hours. Remove the meat from the pot. Strain the liquid. Discard the vegetables. Place the meat back in a clean pot, plus the liquid. Sauté the bacon, mushrooms and onions in the butter. Add to the pot. Reheat the lot. Blend the flour with remaining butter. Stir it into the sauce, stirring well.

- Taste for seasoning. Serve in a deep dish with buttery mash.

Serves: 4

Spring Cabbage with Bacon

Ingredients

1 head of Spring cabbage
2 back rashers, diced
1 onion, finely chopped
75 g butter
Salt and pepper, to taste

Method

- Cut cabbage head in half and slice very finely. Blanch in a little water for 5 minutes and strain.

- Melt the butter in a heavy saucepan. Add chopped onion and rashers. Simmer for 5 minutes.

- Add the blanched cabbage. Stir well, season with salt and pepper and serve.

  Serves: 6–8

Roast Rack of Lamb with Fresh Herbs & Garlic

Ingredients

2 racks of Irish lamb, well trimmed and chined
50 g white breadcrumbs
25 g chopped herbs, thyme, rosemary and parsley
1 clove garlic, crushed
Salt and freshly ground black pepper
25 g melted butter

Method

- Lightly score the meat in a criss-cross pattern to allow the seasonings to permeate the fat and meat.

- Season the rack with salt and pepper and, in a hot pan, seal the meat in melted butter.

- In a bowl, mix all the other ingredients together, so you have a type of dry stuffing.

- Place this on top of the lamb pressing well onto the meat. Place in a hot oven Gas Mark 9, 240°C (475°F), for 30 minutes, longer if you require the meat well done.

- Take from the oven and keep warm. This allows the meat to settle.

To Serve

- Serve with a thin gravy which you can make from the roasting dish juices, some roast potatoes and a green salad.

Serves: 4

Spiced Aubergines

An alternative way to serve Rack of Lamb is with Spiced Aubergines.

Ingredients

1–2 tablespoons oil
2 aubergines, diced
1 teaspoon ground coriander
1 teaspoon turmeric
1 teaspoon cumin
1 fresh chilli, chopped, include the seeds
1 teaspoon fresh ginger, grated
2–3 cloves garlic, chopped
1 can tomatoes, chopped
3 tablespoons sugar
Salt and black pepper, to taste
Vinegar

Method

- Heat the oil in a large pan.

- Add the diced aubergines, sauté for 1–2 minutes then add the coriander, turmeric, cumin, chilli, ginger and garlic.

- Cook for 3–4 minutes over a gentle heat.

- Add the tomatoes, vinegar, sugar and seasoning.

- Stir well and simmer for 20 minutes. Taste for seasoning.

Smoked Salmon on Potato Cakes with Soured Cream

Ingredients

12 slices smoked salmon, brown part removed from centre

Potato Cakes

460 g cooked, mashed potatoes
75 g flour
2 eggs, beaten
2 tablespoons chives, finely chopped
75 ml soured cream

Method

- Mix the potato, flour, egg, scallions, salt, pepper, nutmeg and half the butter. Mix well together and shape into 12 small potato cakes.

- Heat the remaining butter in a non-stick pan, then cook the potato cakes until nicely browned on either side.

- The cakes can be served immediately or kept overnight in the fridge.

- 15 minutes before serving, reheat in the oven.

To Serve

- Mix the soured cream, seasoning and chives together.

- Place the smoked salmon on each potato cake and top with the soured cream and chives.

Serves: 6

Smoked Haddock —
Champ Poached Egg & Chive Sauce

Ingredients

2 x 160 g undyed
    smoked haddock
180 ml fish stock
70 ml dry white wine
130 ml cream
2 teaspoons chives, chopped

2 eggs, poached
Finely chopped spring onions or leeks
180 g mash potato
30 g butter
White wine vinegar

Method

- Have your fishmonger – if you know him well enough and he's friendly – remove all the pin bones from the smoked haddock.

- Poach the fish fillets in fish stock and white wine for 4–5 minutes (simmer very slowly).

- Remove the fish and keep warm.

- Strain the stock and simmer over a high heat until reduced by half or more, add the cream and reduce again until the sauce begins to thicken, add the chopped chives.

- Poach the eggs in boiling water and white wine vinegar until soft poached, then drain.

- Mix the spring onion or lightly cooked leeks with mashed potato, add butter.

- Place a mound of champ on each plate, place fish fillet on top (remove skin, if possible), place poached egg on top and pour over the chive sauce.

Serves: 2

Veal or Beef or Lamb Stock

Ingredients

2 kg bones
200 g carrots
200 g onions
2 leeks
2 shallots
1 clove garlic, chopped
1 bouquet garni (thyme, parsley, bay leaf)
6 l water

Method

@› Heat oven to Gas Mark 10, 260°C (500°F).

@› Put the bones into a roasting dish in the oven and roast until dark brown.

@› Peel and chop the vegetables. Add them to the roasting dish, when the bones are already half browned.

@› Put the browned bones and vegetables into a large saucepan, with the garlic and bouquet garni. Add enough water to cover the bones generously. Bring slowly to the boil, skimming whenever fat forms on the surface.

@› Continue cooking gently, uncovered, for 4 hours.

@› Skim when necessary and, if need be, add a little water during cooking so the bones remain covered.

@› Strain the stock.

@› After the stock has been strained, reduce it until less than one-third remains, 2 litres of stock.

Quantity: Makes 2 litres

A watercolour of John Howard by Claire Cryan

Fish Stock

Ingredients

2 kg sole or turbot bones if possible, otherwise use whatever
    white fish bones you can get
1 litre dry white wine
1 litre water
1 onion, studded with a clove
1 bouquet garni (leek, carrot, celery, parsley and bay leaf)

Method

- Soak the bones in running cold water for one hour.

- Chop them into pieces.

- Put in a saucepan with the wine and water.

- Bring slowly to the boil, reduce to simmer and skim frequently.

- When skimming is complete, add the bouquet garni and cook gently for 30–40 minutes.

- Strain the stock, then return to a clean saucepan and continue to simmer until the stock has reduced to 1 litre.

Quantity : Makes 1 litre

Chicken Stock

All stocks can be kept in the freezer. For home use, make 1 litre. (Note: freeze stock in small quantities – they are more useful this way.)

Ingredients

1 chicken and giblets
1 onion, studded with a clove
1 leek
1 stick celery
1 clove garlic, crushed
100 g carrots
1 bouquet garni
3 litres water
Salt

Method

- Wash, peel and coarsely chop all the vegetables.

- At the same time, start cooking the chicken and giblets in cold unsalted water. Bring to the boil and add the vegetables, garlic and bouquet garni. Continue cooking for 3 hours, skimming frequently.

- Carefully remove the chicken. The meat can be used as a stuffing for vegetables, croquettes or salad.

- Strain the stock through a sieve in which you have laid a dampened muslin cloth.

- Season very lightly with salt and allow to cool.

  Quantity: Makes 2.5 litres

Creme Brulée with Ginger & Brown Bread Ice Cream

Ingredients

½ litre of double cream
3 egg yolks
100 g castor sugar
Vanilla pod or vanilla essence, if required
Brown sugar
Fresh ginger, finely grated

Method

- Bring ¾ double cream to the boil and remove from the heat. Mix the rest of the cream, the egg yolks, castor sugar and ginger thoroughly together. Add to the boiling cream, add the vanilla. Return to the heat and stir constantly with a wooden spoon until just at boiling point. Remove from the heat and pour into 4 Ramekin dishes. Allow to cool and set.

- Sprinkle each dish with brown sugar and glaze quickly under a salamander or use a blow torch. Return to the refrigerator and allow to set.

To Serve

- Serve and with some brown bread ice cream and a shortbread biscuit, if required.

Serves: 4

Brown Bread Ice Cream

Ingredients

150 g stale brown breadcrumbs
150 g dark brown sugar
2 tablespoons sugar
100 ml water
2 egg yolks
½ teaspoon vanilla essence
500 ml whipped cream

Method

- Combine the breadcrumbs and brown sugar and place in a hot oven to crispen and carmelise well.

- Boil the sugar and water together to a thread. It will look thick and syrupy and when a spoon is dipped in, the last drops of syrup will form thin threads. Beat this a little at a time into the egg yolks. Add vanilla essence and beat to a thick creamy white mousse. Fold the cream in. Then add the cooled carmelised breadcrumbs and brown sugar mixture. Set to freeze.

Serves: 6–8

Hazlenut Soufflé

Ingredients

Soufflé

½ litre milk
50 g flour
40 g butter
30 g hazelnuts, toasted and chopped
6 egg yolks
5 egg whites
100 g sugar

Sauce

Lightly whipped cream
Hazlenut liquor
10 g pralined hazelnuts

- Mix all ingredients together.

Soufflé Method

- Boil the milk, make *beurre manié* with the flour and butter and use to thicken the milk, add hazelnuts and egg yolks and take off the heat. Fold stiffly beaten egg whites into this mixture.

- Pour the mixture into buttered and sugared moulds. Bake for 15 minutes in a moderate oven. Serve hot with sauce poured on top of the soufflé.

Serves: 6 cuts

Fishing for oysters

With head chef, Jimmy O'Sullivan

At a competition in the Netherlands (left to right),
John Morrin, John, and the late Michael Marley

Apple & Jameson Tart

Ingredients

250 g shortcrust pastry
50 g ground almonds
4 large Bramley apples,
   peeled and diced
2 tablespoons sugar

250 ml cream
3 egg yolks
50 g caster sugar
Dash of Jameson whiskey

To Cook

- Set the oven to Gas Mark 6, 200°C (400°F).

- Line 4 individual tart tins with the pastry. Sprinkle some ground almonds on the base of each one. Then add the apple and enough sugar to sweeten.

- Heat the cream. Beat the egg yolks and sugar together. Stir in the cream and a dash of whiskey. Spoon a little of the cream mixture into each tart. Keep remaining cream. Bake tarts for 25–35 minutes.

- Pour the remaining cream into a bowl. Place over simmering water. Stirring constantly, continue to cook until the custard thickens. Set aside – keep warm.

To Serve

- Serve the tart, dusted with icing sugar, with the warm custard. Vanilla ice-cream, thin almond biscuit, raspberries, etc. are optional.

Serves: 4 individual tarts

Rhubarb Crumble Tart

Ingredients

450 g flour
250 g butter
50 g caster sugar
2 free-range egg yolks

Pastry

- Set oven at Gas Mark 6, 200°C (400°F).

- Sieve the flour into a mixing bowl and rub in the butter until the mixture resembles fine breadcrumbs. Add the sugar, beat the egg yolks with two teaspoons of cold water. Use the egg mixture to bind the pastry, adding a little more water if necessary to form a soft, not sticky, dough.

- Knead on a lightly floured surface and use to line baking tins. Line the pastry with greaseproof paper and fill with baking beans. Bake blind for 15 minutes. Remove from the oven and discard the paper, save the beans for another day.

Pastry makes 12 x 10 cm tarts

Rhubarb Filling

1 kg rhubarb, chopped
100 g brown sugar

- Place rhubarb and brown sugar in a saucepan. Soften over a gentle heat and allow to cool.

Crumble

150 g flour
100 g butter
50 g porridge oats
100 g brown sugar

 Combine all the ingredients in a bowl.

To Assemble

 Set oven at Gas Mark 4, 180°C (350°F).

 Divide the cooled rhubarb mixture between the pastry cases and sprinkle the crumble over. Cook for 15–20 minutes until the topping is golden brown.

To Serve

 Serve with crème anglaise and brown bread ice cream.

Wholewheat Bread

Ingredients

680 g wholemeal flour (Howard's Wholemeal)
120 g white flour
100 g porridge oats
60 g bran
175 g pinhead oatmeal
60 g wheatgerm
½ teaspoon baking powder
½ teaspoon sea salt
2 eggs, beaten
1.2 l buttermilk

Method

- Mix all the dry ingredients together in a large bowl and make a well in the centre.

- Add the eggs and milk to the well in the dry ingredients and gradually incorporate the dry ingredients into the liquid until all is well blended.

- Spoon into 2 greased 500 g loaf tins and bake in the centre of an oven preheated to Gas Mark 4, 180°C (350°F) for 1¼–1½ hours. When cooked, the loaves should sound hollow when tapped underneath.

- Turn out the tins to cool on a wire rack.

4 Charles J. Haughey at Le Coq Hardi

*There is more simplicity in the man who eats
Caviar on impulse than in the man who eats
Grapenuts on principle.*

G.K. Chesterton

*To be miserly towards your friends is not pretty;
To be miserly towards yourself is contemptible.*

Norman Douglas

*O*f the many regular and loyal patrons of the restaurant, few attracted as much attention to it as did Charles J. Haughey. My own first personal encounter with Charles Haughey was in the private dining room of the restaurant. The first-floor room was elegantly furnished and hung with good, quality Irish paintings. The atmosphere was that of a gentleman's club. A highly polished mahogany table was set with silver flatware, fine bone china and stiff linen napery. Leather-bound books filled two alcoves on either side of a white marble chimneypiece. A three-decanter Tantalus sitting on a bookcase was missing one of its cut glass receptacles. Apparently, it had fallen victim to a boisterous night's revelry in the distant past. The room was reflected in a heavy gilt overmantel.

All of this was several years before the word "tribunal" had become a household word in Ireland. I had been solidly warned to be punctual because the former Taoiseach believed firmly in the dictate "punctuality is the politeness of princes". At this time, Mr Haughey was at the very height of his popularity. He had achieved the heady rank of elder statesman and rumours were circulating of his intention to seek election to the presidency of Ireland. However, it had also been humorously rumoured that he was not interested in the job because he did not relish moving to a smaller house!

Looking out of the window, I saw the dark-blue state Mercedes enter the driveway. His driver remained in the car, while the sprightly figure in navy blazer and check shirt with open collar alighted quickly from the front passenger seat and made his way up the granite steps. I observed that he was not wearing a tie. His television statesman's image always seemed to come with the obligatory necktie. Only on his private yacht, *Celtic Mist,* or ambling about his demesne did he appear in casual attire, or so it seemed to me, observing his life from the distance of the television screen. I removed my own tie and stuffed it in my pocket. I thought a little informality might go a long way, and I did not wish to seem over formal when a former Prime Minister obviously thought this was a casual lunch.

I was standing by the chimneypiece in the upstairs room when the familiar figure and voice of the ex-Taoiseach was ushered in by the headwaiter. "I see you're on your own" was his opening remark as he extended his hand in a rather peculiar way. It appeared to come at me from above. A friend, who is a tower of trivia, later told me that Napoleon had the same gesture. He had no explanation

View from the private dining room

A Christmas gift from Charles J. Haughey
to Catherine Howard

The private dining room

Charles J. Haughey

as to the reason for it, but said it had something to do with creating first impressions. I have no idea what Desmond Morris would make of it. The presence standing before me could not have been more imposing. I had seen him at close quarter in the Dáil and at numerous press conferences but this was my first encounter of a close personal kind. "Yes, I am on my own, sir." I found myself adding the "sir" not as a residual act of sycophancy, but because it seemed correct to address a former head of government in this way. It immediately seemed to have hit the right note with him. He had a particular aversion to calling journalists by their first name and regularly berated his ministers for this habit, which he claimed created a sense of over familiarity, particularly for television audiences.

He suggested a glass of champagne. "Veuve Clicquot," he directed to the waiter who left the room with a courteous bow of the head. "Ah, the 'widow'," I said, not really being sure as to how he would react to my knowing the colloquial name for this brand of champagne. The steely gaze of those famous hooded eyes met me with mesmeric full-on intensity and just for a moment, I thought the remark had instantly upset my meeting with this political legend. "Good man," he said to my welcome relief, "you must be the only person in RTÉ to know that." He enjoyed having the occasional swipe at the media and RTÉ was a favourite target for his ire. He once described an *Irish Times* editorial rather graphically as being like "an auld one sitting in the bath with the water growing cold around her fanny". There was conviviality in the air as we chatted about Séan Lemass.

As another waiter entered the room carrying the champagne, Charles Haughey now turned and addressed him in French. This is a gesture the French always welcome, but I had a feeling from something this obvious polyglot said to me before my host arrived that he was, in fact, Portuguese. As the two men exchanged further pleasantries in French, my mind wandered to a famous occasion when Mr Haughey as Taoiseach entertained members of his Cabinet to luncheon. After the menu had been consulted by all, the waiter asked the Taoiseach what he wished to have as his main course. He chose beef. "And the vegetables, sir?" asked the waiter. Haughey, looking straight at his ministers who were still consulting their menus, said "they'll have the same". Apocryphal or not, it has the ring of a true Haughey story.

I was determined that there would be no such indignity visited on my head, so I manoeuvred the opening conversation around to food and wine.

Having spent a great deal of time and the majority of my inheritance on fine dining and cavorting, I was well placed to give him a run for his money on these subjects. He displayed a huge and authoritative knowledge of French wine, especially the top end clarets. A 1982 Chateau Calon-Segur was ordered. "Two bottles and
decant them now please." We were beginning to discuss the so-called "Wild
Geese" wines – the wines with an Irish family association like Talbot, Kirwan,
Dillon, when the door was opened to admit the other luncheon guest, who arrived
slightly but elegantly breathless, moving across the room to greet our host with
"sorry, I'm late sweetie, but I couldn't get away from the office". The other guest
was journalist Terry Keane.

In fact, I owed my meeting with Charles Haughey to Terry Keane.
She arranged it soon after I told her that I had been commissioned to write a biography of Mr Haughey's father-in-law, former Taoiseach Seán Lemass. I had met
Mrs Keane on the evening of my thirty-third birthday. After a birthday dinner host-
ed by friends, we made our way to the private bar of the then fashionable POD
nightclub on Harcourt Street and there I was introduced to her by Donal McNally
of Optica, who was in the company of Terry's friend Tom Kennedy of Alias Tom.

She asked me directly "what do you do" and I recall saying rather
curtly "about what?"

"For a crust," she pressed. I told her I was writing a biography of
the President of Ireland, Mary Robinson, that I was a journalist on the Foreign
Desk at RTÉ and that I had returned from Vienna where I had worked as a foreign
correspondent for the London *Independent.* Robinson, rather than RTÉ or Vienna,
seemed to interest her and she launched into a series of hilarious, gloriously dis-
respectful stories about the President, whom she had known for many years
through her husband, Judge Ronan Keane.

Mrs Keane, then a legendary diarist and fashion columnist, was a
captivating presence and one of the wittiest and most engaging women in Ireland.
She had a loyal band of close friends and no shortage of enemies acquired through
her gossip column in the *Sunday Independent.* As the evening progressed and the
champagne flowed, she invited me to lunch the next day with the enticing prom-
ise of further revelations on "Her Poloness" as she called Mrs Robinson.
We agreed to meet at my flat. At one o'clock precisely, the doorbell rang. I was still

in bed nursing a crippling birthday hangover. "I'm frightfully sorry," I blurted out as I struggled to open the door still in my dressing gown. "Will you have a glass of champagne?"

Several hours later, after a riveting and highly liquid lunch in a restaurant, the name of which now escapes me – though I do recall it was on Harcourt Street and has since closed – we linked one another arm in arm across St Stephen's Green and settled in for a drink, served by the genial Seán Boyd in the welcoming darkness of the Shelbourne's Horseshoe Bar. A new friendship, which took us to London, Prague, South Africa, France and all over Ireland, had begun. Also, it had an understanding that brought me face to face with Charles Haughey in the private dining room of *Le Coq Hardi*.

A great deal of nonsense has been written about how much of their affair was conducted in the intimate opulence of the private dining room of the restaurant. The tales ran the full gamut of sordid tabloid invention. There were inaccurate reports of the chandeliers in the downstairs main dining room shaking from the vigorous lovemaking which went on above. The truth was otherwise. The most strenuous activity taking place upstairs was the pulling of champagne corks!

Few who experienced his hospitality would doubt that Mr Haughey was a generous and gracious host. The question of where the money for this largesse came from is not the concern of this particular book. Most people at the time, including myself, assumed that he had considerable private income but very few knew its source. Judging it retrospectively only brings on unnecessary indigestion and Judgement has been passed elsewhere.

On that first meeting, as we made our way to the table our host had already worked out the placement. "Would you kindly sit there with your back to the window," he said to me. The position, to my surprise, was at the head of the table. Mrs Keane was on my right, the former Taoiseach on my left. He looked at me with a half smile and said "I put you there so that you can take the bullet." Most reassuring, I thought. John Howard also recalled that whenever he was asked to come to the private dining room, CJH would pull down the blind if they were standing by the window. This was all done in a well-practised gesture of "send up" and faux conspiracy.

Menus were produced again. The conversation turned to oysters, about which our host knew a very great deal. There was some joke about the oyster's curious sexuality and the fact that it spends most of its life in bed resting on its left side and is protected by Acts of Parliament. Its alleged aphrodisiac qualities were not touched upon, but the almost Swiftian fact that it often absorbs its own young was. I mentioned the fact that the ancient Greeks used the oyster shell as a voting counter in parliament, a fact which seemed to amuse my host. He did not seem amused by Dr Johnson's description of them as "children's ears in sawdust", but chuckled at the wise observation of King James I, which runs: "He was a brave man who first swallowed an oyster." La Fontaine's "The Oyster and the Litigants" was also mentioned and I recall there was very little sympathy for the lawyer in the following tale:

The Oyster and the Litigants

One day two travellers, walking side by side,
Came on an oyster washed up by the tide.
Greedily they devoured it with their eyes,
Excitedly they pointed out its size,
And then, inevitably, they faced
The problem: which of them as judge
Should pass a verdict on the taste?
One was already stooping for the prize
When his friend gave him a nudge:
'We must decide this properly.
The epicure's monopoly
Belongs to whoever saw it first: *he* swallows
The oyster and, it logically follows,
The other has to watch him do it.'
'If that's the way you view it,
I have, thank God, remarkably keen sight.'
'Mine's pretty good as well,
And upon my life I swear

I saw it before you!' 'So what? All right,
You may have been
The first to *see,* but I was the first to *smell.*
Who should arrive upon this charming scene
But Perrin Dandin? Asked to intervene
As arbiter in the affair,
With a portentous air
He digs the oysters from its shell
And gulps it while his audience stands and stares.
The meal finished, he declares
In the tone of voice beloved of presidents:
'The court hereby decrees
An award, without costs, of one shell to each.
Both parties please
Proceed without a breach
Of the peace to your lawful residence.'
Count what it costs these days to go to court,
And how little the families driven to that resort
Have left after expenses. It's the Law,
It's Perrin Dandin who eats up the rest –
Who takes the wing and breast
And leaves the litigants the beak and claw.

*****

Oddly enough, after extolling the virtues of the native Irish oyster, we all went on to order something entirely different. I had never before heard of the famous Coq Hardi Smokies and they were recommended to me with such reverential gusto that I thought to refuse them would appear an act of singular churlishness. This was a delicious smoked fish dish, which John Howard had turned into one of the hallmark first courses of the restaurant. It has since been imitated in many other establishments. (The recipe appears on page 38.)

It had often been mentioned to me, erroneously as it turned out in my experience, that my host spent vast sums of money on expensive wines from the renowned wine list of the restaurant. It contained some of the great classics, the price of which, for the average person, would represent a second mortgage even in those days when Irish houses were affordable. Charles Haughey selected well but not ostentatiously or expensively. I soon realised that he preferred to discover something good that represented value rather than splash out on showy big names.

Only once, during a lunch for two English friends of mine, did I witness him break his usual habit and spend £500 on a bottle of 1967 Château d'Yquem. One of the guests was a wine critic for a major British newspaper and the wine in question is a legend of its type. A spectacular gesture and a truly spectacular wine.

Over the next few years, I dined intermittently with Charles Haughey at *Le Coq Hardi*. The pattern rarely varied. Be it lunch or dinner, he arrived on time and left early. If it was a Monday luncheon, he left at 2.30 pm for his weekly doctor's appointment. If it was dinner, I rarely recollect him staying in the restaurant after midnight. He did however insist that his bill remained open, so that guests who wished to remain on after he left could enjoy his hospitality without his being present. I never saw this gesture abused. *Noblesse oblige.*

Charles Haughey's reverence for all things French was very noticeable when he dined at *Le Coq Hardi*. When Ireland held the European presidency in 1989, he was anxious that the Heads of State lunch in Dublin Castle would be an exercise in culinary perfection. He asked John Howard to cook for his distinguished guests. The menu consisted of Fricassée of Wild Irish Mushrooms with a Salad of Mixed Baby Leaves, Consommé of Guinea Fowl with Truffles, Rack of Wicklow Lamb, and Summer Pudding. The wines were Montrachet, Lynch Bages 1982, Château d'Yquem 1967, Hennessy X.O and Dom Pérignon 1976. The Taoiseach tested each dish before the menu was agreed. When the event ran late and it was feared that dinner would be jeopardised, a garda escort was provided for the staff of *Le Coq Hardi* to get to the next venue, Malahide Castle. The event was put in jeopardy when the gardaí nearly arrested Catherine Howard when she was found making her way hastily through the hotel gardens with a box. She was asked to verify her date of birth and this

In Ómós
Uachtarán Phoblacht na hOstaire
A Shoilse Thomas Klestil
ar Ócáid a Chuairte ar Éirinn

In honour of
The President of the Austrian Republic
His Excellency Thomas Klestil
on the Occasion of his Visit to Ireland

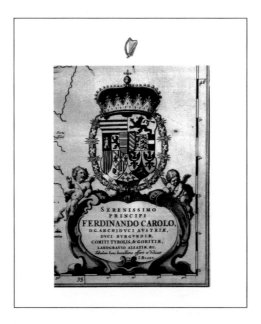

Menu for the State dinner in honour of
the President of Austria

was then relayed by Garda radio all over Ireland. The box contained nothing more dangerous than sets of white cotton gloves for her waiting staff!

Charles Haughey and François Mitterand became quite good friends. As the old French president lay dying of cancer in December 1995, he invited friends to a final meal. A friend of mine reading of the event remarked how Haugheyesque the scene was, and wondered aloud how he thought the former Taoiseach would have approved. It was the French President's Last Supper. It consisted of oysters followed by *foie gras* then roast capon and finally a forbidden, indeed an illegal dish – roast *ortolan,* known in this part of the world as the tiny songbird, the bunting. It must be captured alive, then blinded or kept in complete darkness and force-fed on grain, grapes and figs until it reaches four times its normal size. It is then drowned in Armagnac or cognac and roasted for about seven minutes.

The real skill is in the eating of the bird. The diners' head is covered with a cloth. This is to conceal from God the act of gluttony that is about to take place. The *ortolan* is placed in the mouth with its head protruding. The head is then bitten off and the carcass chewed completely. The release of flavours which then takes places is said to be one of the greatest gastronomic experiences known to carnivores. Aficionados claim they can taste the wheat of Morocco, the sea air of the Mediterranean and all the other flavours that are released during the fifteen minutes it takes to chew the tiny bird. When Mitterand was having his Last Supper, he was so weak from cancer that he is said to have passed out between courses. Though there is a massive fine for breaking the law prohibiting the killing of the *ortolan,* the former French President ate two and died a week later without eating another morsel. Surely, it gives new meaning to going out in style. On the other hand, as Bertolt Brecht would have it "grub first: then ethics".

Charles Haughey marked many of the triumphs and at least two of the low points of his public and private life in *Le Coq Hardi.* When he finally decided to leave office as Taoiseach, he sought out the comfort of his favourite restaurant. In lively company, he dined on wild mushrooms and asparagus and a game dish. He rarely ate puddings, despite his passion for good-quality chocolate. Over a modest consumption of wine that night, friends recall that the sealing of his fate appeared to be a burden lifted as his life in public office drew to a close.

Over the next few years, and before the various tribunal revelations, Charles Haughey began to enjoy his favourite Dublin restaurant in a more relaxed way. The walls of *Le Coq Hardi*'s private dining room would witness one last turbulent moment – the finale to his relationship with Terry Keane. Over lunch, it is understood, she informed him of her decision to go public about their relationship in the Irish edition of the *Sunday Times* and on RTÉ's *Late Late Show.* Mere speculation, not history, records Mr Haughey's reaction. Charles Haughey never again dined at *Le Coq Hardi.*

5 Tales from the Cellar

Claret is a drink for boys, Port for men, but he
Who aspires to being a hero must drink Brandy.
Samuel Johnson

Water for Oxen, Wine for Kings.
Spanish proverb

It's a Naïve Domestic Burgundy, Without Any
Breeding, But I think You'll be Amused by its
Presumption.
Cartoon caption
from James Thurber

here are few restaurants in the world that can boast a Carte de Vin that contains the vertical list of Château Mouton-Rothschild from 1945. *Le Coq Hardi* could make such a boast. However, John Howard was proud rather than boastful about the contents of his cellar. His first review as chef-patron in 1977 gently admonished him for the uninspired quality of his wine list. He resolved thereafter that such a situation would never obtain in any establishment owned by him. He set about acquainting himself with a knowledge of wine that eventually led to his owning a cellar of world class and quality. *Le Coq Hardi's* list became something of a legend and was epic in terms of the choice it offered. It came to the table in a leather-bound volume that rivalled the Dublin telephone directory in size and appearance. It contained over 700 different wines that ranged from a Château Mouton-Rothschild 1870 which cost just under £5,000 a bottle, to a more affordable Bourgogne AC, Cuvée Louis Latour at £15. There was a magical world of wine in the bins in between.

Despite being in possession of such a superb and impressive list, John Howard rarely advised patrons to push the boat out on spending unconscionable sums on wine. He preferred the focus to be on his food. Spending large showy sums on wine in restaurants has long been considered a vulgarity associated with "new" money. The ability to choose a wine from a restaurant's list, which matches the quality and style of the food, is a far greater social skill than the ability to sign a credit card slip accounting a four-figure sum for wine. A true connoisseur, in quest of something special must always be allowed licence to break such rules because, invariably, it will be done with discernment and not ostentation in mind. Even the great Robert Parker advises that it is unnecessary to spend huge sums on wine to be sure of drinking something of quality.

There were occasional, terrifying moments when the chef-patron of *Le Coq Hardi* served some of his "treasures of the cellar" to customers whom he feared might reject them on a whim. On a particular evening when a regular diner ordered a bottle of Gruaud-Larose 1961, John stood by waiting for what he hoped would be uncontested approbation. As he tasted the wine, the gentleman looked at him and regaled him with a story of how he had recently returned from a few days profitable racing at Ascot. He sipped a little more. "I must tell you, John that I had dinner at the Connaught in London last night and I sent back a bottle of 1961 Gruaud-Larose."

John's heart sank as he asked "and how is my wine?" The customer took another draught, paused, looked him straight in the eye and said, "Perfect, quite perfect, I think you had better decant another bottle, in fact why not make it two!"

On another occasion, a party of ten Russians came to the restaurant from Killiney Castle. Over dinner, they drank quite a respectable sampling of the Mouton and Latour in the range of £300 to £400 per bottle. The next day, Sunday, John received a call at home from an accountant who had dined with the Russians. Fearing the worst, he immediately thought he was facing a possible complaint about food poisoning or a dispute over the bill. To his intense relief, he was instead asked if he would consider selling the Russians a bottle of 1870 Château Mouton-Rothschild which they had spotted on his list. The asking price was just under £5,000 for this rare and most desirable bottle. John explained the rarity value of the wine, how it had been rebottled during its long life, to expect sediment and the need for decanting. A car was dispatched and the bottle made its way to the airport where the Russian private jet was standing by. An hour later John took another call at home. It was the Russians again. They were delayed at the airport and asked if they could drink the wine there and then. So it was that one of the world's rarest and most expensive wines was consumed on a whim at Dublin Airport. John later sold another bottle of the 1870 to the Mandarin Hotel in Hong Kong. It was a present for a baby boy. History does not record if he consumed it with the same haste as the Russians.

With a view to satisfying the tastes and pockets of all his customers, John travelled extensively and sourced wines from the Old and New Worlds. He also promoted the so-called Irish Chateaux. These were the wines produced by the descendants of the "Wild Geese" whose ancestors had left Ireland after the defeat of the old Gaelic order at the Battle of Kinsale. Wines bearing the names Dillon, McCarthy, Lynch, Barton, Boyd, Phelan, and the great Hennessy Cognac were all represented on the wine list of *Le Coq Hardi.* So too was the latest of the Irish producers to establish a vineyard in France. David O'Brien, son of the legendary trainer, Vincent O'Brien, bought Château Vignelaure in Aix-en-Provence. It had a reputation for the methods of organic production used there. On the list John described David's wine as "the nearest thing to a Bordeaux in Provence". A 1986 Château Vignelaure cost a reasonable £25.

John sought out quality and value while remaining loyal to his own individual taste. He favours Meursaults and Montrachets when it comes to the big Burgundy whites and, in red, he invariably favours claret over all else. However, he admires the efforts of the Rhône Valley producers and shippers such as Guigal and Louis Chave. He rates highly Louis Metaireau, of whose Muscadets he very much approves. Indeed, John regrets that the wines of Alsace are still somewhat neglected in Ireland and elsewhere. It is difficult to beat a good dry Riesling, Gewürztraminer, Pinot Blanc, or Tokay-Pinot Gris from this wonderful region. A good Gerwürztraminer with roast goose was one of the legendary marriages made at *Le Coq Hardi*.

I recall introducing a senior Korean diplomat to this combination at his first luncheon at *Le Coq Hardi* and he still mentions his gratitude in his Christmas greetings to me. This wine is also excellent with *foie gras* or with a rich blue cheese. A recent and sensible trend recommended stoutly by Robert Parker is the use of white wine to accompany cheese. It has the effect of cutting the edge off the high-fat content of many cheeses and leaves one with an altogether happier digestive system, especially after late evening dining.

John has long been a supporter of the wines produced by Domaine Zind-Humbrecht. Their Tokay-Pinot Gris can give Montrachet a very decent run for its money. It is worth remembering that, especially in Ireland, the wines of Alsace do not move at lightning speed off the wine merchants' shelves. Do not despair at the age of some of them because they have a longer shelf life than many whites and, therefore, some extraordinary bargains are to be had. Well-cellared bottles of the 1967s, 1971s and 1976s in Rieslings and Gewürztraminers are a testament to the aging potential of these fabulous white wines, and it is surprising how often they are treated with scant respect. Should you be fortunate enough to see any strays, be sure to round them up. John Howard advised customers and friends to lay down the wines of the 1980s. This decade was a truly great one for claret, producing vintages in 1982, 1983, 1985, 1986, 1989, and then 1990.

We inherited from the English the tradition of port drinking and the rituals that go with it. *Le Coq Hardi* had a superb collection of ports. It is rare for more than four vintages to be declared for port in any one decade. Some of the greatest vintages of the twentieth century are 1912, 1927, 1931, 1935, 1945,

Sommelier Nicholas Allas

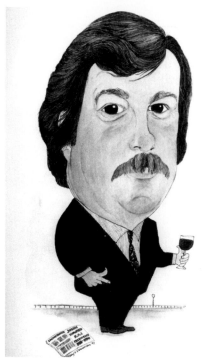

A cartoon presented to John on the occasion of his presidency of the Restaurants Association of Ireland

1948, 1955, 1963, 1970, 1977, 1983, 1985 and 1992. A vintage is declared the second spring after the harvest and a vintage port can improve and survive for up to fifty years and beyond. A tip to remember. Do not eat oysters and drink port at the same meal. They are not easy bedfellows and the effects can be very nasty. If you feel you have had a bad oyster, throw back a shot of Calvados. That should keep the offending oyster in its rightful place. John Howard recalls that *Le Coq Hardi* did not sell great quantities of port.

He advised clients and friends that the ports of the 1980s were good investments for the cellar. Quite a few of the patrons of the restaurant kept good cellars and relied on John for sensible advice. Some were sensible; others saw the cellar as a place for high jinks. I once saw the following amusing Limerick pinned on the door of a well-stocked private cellar in Dublin:

> My God! He's an impudent fella!
> – That girl that he showed round the cellar
> Lost her *status quo ante*
> Between the Chianti
> And the magnums of Valpolicella ...
> Which reminds me of Asti Spumante,
> A wine that I'm more *pro* than *anti* –
> The only thing is
> This aphrodisiac fizz
> Leads to *delicto flagrante* ...

Wine writers and merchants offering high-sounding advice on the laying down of a good cellar have lost us acres of rainforest in the process. Auberon Waugh wrote one of the better articles on the contents of a cellar; about that of his father Evelyn Waugh. I include it here because Waugh came to Ireland looking for a house and it might have been written about an Irish cellar because it was the main feature he admired in several houses he visited. It's also a wonderful piece of impish writing from the pen of the late editor of *The Literary Review*. Through the kindness of Berry Brothers and Rudd in whose house magazine, *Number Three, St James's Street*, it first appeared, we are pleased to reproduce it here.

My Father's Cellar

Auberon Waugh

For a man whose life revolved around wine, Evelyn Waugh wrote surprisingly little on the subject. Even his novels have few references to this lifelong passion, although there is a famous passage from *Brideshead Revisited,* when Charles Ryder, staying with his friend Sebastian, 'first made a serious acquaintance with wine and sowed the seed of that rich harvest which was to be my stay in many barren years'. Many will remember the scene when they sit up late in the Painted Parlour, getting their glasses more and more muddled as their praise for the wine grows wilder and more exotic:

'... It is a little shy wine like a gazelle.'
'Like a leprechaun.'
'Dappled, in a tapestry meadow.'
'Like a flute by still water.'
'... And this is a wise old wine.'
'A prophet in a cave.'
'... And this is a necklace of pearls on a white neck.'
'Like a swan.'
'Like the last unicorn ...'
'Ought we to be drunk *every* night?'
Sebastian asked one morning.
'Yes, I think so.'
'I think so too.'

Goodness knows how many sottish late-night conversations that passage has inspired among later generations of Oxford undergraduates, but I feel it belongs among the immortal pieces of wine writing, along with Thurber's famous captions, from *Men, Women and Dogs:* 'It's a Naïve Domestic Burgundy, Without Any Breeding, But I Think You'll be Amused by its Presumption.'

One might also deduce from the scarcity of Evelyn Waugh's writing about wine that it belonged to that part of his life which he regarded as private. The fierceness with which he defended his own privacy gave rise to many of the stories – gossip columns were full of them – which portrayed him as a monstrous old blimp, roaring and yelling at any intruder into his private domain. In fact he was a gentle, humorous man – sometimes sad, sometimes gloomy – and nowhere near as bad-tempered as he appeared to the Press and public on his few excursions outside the small world of family and friends. But I do not think it is betraying a trust to reveal an aspect of his private life which will be of great interest to wine-drinkers and which has never, so far as I know, been revealed before.

The mid-life crisis is familiar among males in our society. Many mark it by leaving their wives of many years and taking up with some luscious young dolly bird or, if they are not married (like Bernard Levin) they may give up their work and go to live at an ashram in Poona. Evelyn Waugh celebrated his own mid-life crisis first of all by going mad soon after his 50th birthday, in January 1954. This episode is well documented in his novel, *The Ordeal of Gilbert Pinfold,* first published in 1957 but available in Penguin. Next, having recovered his sanity, he sold his house and moved to the huge icebox at Combe Florey, in Somerset, where I now live. In the process, he suffered a violent change in his wine-drinking habits which was to remain with him for the rest of his life – he died in 1966 – as the only permanent trauma from his experiences at this time. From that moment, he could *never touch a drop of claret,* in any circumstances.

It would be interesting to know if others have had the same experience in middle age. His house in Gloucestershire was famous for the excellence of its clarets – as for its vintage ports – but just before moving house, in the late autumn of 1956, he sold every bottle of claret in his cellar, and never bought another. Worse than this, he could not bring himself to drink any red wine from Bordeaux even in the house of friends. A year ago I found myself sitting next to Sir Hugh Greene, the former Director General of the BBC. Like the Ancient Mariner, he held me with his skinny hand and told me a tale of woe which had understandably been haunting him for years. It appeared that at some time in the early 1960s, probably 1963, Evelyn Waugh had visited the BBC to make a broadcast about P.G. Wodehouse, and Greene had decided to give a dinner party at

Broadcasting House. In Waugh's honour, Greene had procured rather a special bottle of claret – not just rather a special bottle, but the classic, never-to-be-forgotten Cheval Blanc 1947. Evelyn Waugh thanked him very much, but declined to take any. End of story.

Plainly, this violent repudiation of the world's second best wine-producing area was the result of some psychological trauma, if not actual brain damage. He was quite happy to experiment with wines from unlikely places like Chile (probably of Cabernet base, although in those days they did not specify the grape) and once discovered a new enthusiasm for the red wines of Germany. Even more shaming than that, he came back from Rhodesia one day announcing a new discovery from Portugal called Mateus Rosé, and drank it through one whole summer. Whenever challenged with this, I loyally maintain that the Mateus Rosé of the late '50s was a quite different wine from the sugary pink fizz of today, but I do not honestly know where the truth lies. (See Sacheverell Sitwell's 'Discovery' of Mateus Rosé, which must have been before 1951, p. 42.)

At any rate, no claret ever entered the cellar at Combe Florey until 1971, when I moved back. At Evelyn Waugh's death in 1966 he left four or five dozen Chambertin 1955 from Berry Bros. – a magnificent wine, but one which would have improved with keeping in less frigid surroundings than the cellars at Combe Florey. Although, so far as I know, no wine has ever actually frozen solid down there, I cannot think why not, as the temperature in his day was frequently below freezing point. He also had two cases of Richebourg from Berrys' – I think the vintage was also 1955 – some odd parcels of rather old Sauternes, notably Suduiraut 1947, and a lot of champagne, notably Clicquot Rosé for which he had developed an old man's passion. There were no bottles of vintage port and nothing else.

I think I may have one clue, which is neither psychological nor biochemical, for Evelyn Waugh's repudiation of claret. For some reason, he always referred to it as 'clart', even in such homely expressions as 'to tap the claret', meaning to draw blood in a fight. 'Have a glass of clart,' he would say. Some had difficulty in understanding what he meant, but he persisted. Then in 1956 there was published a rather shameful book called *Noblesse Oblige,* edited by Nancy Mitford, with contributions from herself, Waugh, John Betjeman, Christopher Sykes and others, discussing the characteristics of the English upper class. In the course of his contribution, Sykes – who was a friend of my father's, despite being, as he frequently pointed out, of better breeding – mentioned 'a Gloucestershire landowner' who believed 'that persons of family always refer to the wines of Bordeaux as "clart", to rhyme with cart'. Mr Sykes opined that 'this delusion' showed 'an impulse towards gentility' which might be preferable to the contrary impulse, among true aristocrats, towards affecting the mannerisms of the proletariat.

My father spotted the reference to himself immediately, and although he took it in good part, it must have left him in something of a quandary. Either he had to drop his harmless affectation in deference to the mockery of a younger man and lesser artist, which he did not deign to do, or he had to persist in the awareness that everyone was sniggering at him as the Gloucestershire landowner who said 'clart' when he meant 'claret'. I do not know how much influence it had on his subsequent behaviour, but it is a fact that within a year he had sold not only his house in Gloucestershire but also all his claret, and never touched the stuff again.

I cannot leave the subject without touching on Evelyn Waugh's wine-writing such as it was. His main contribution to the field (I exclude his work on a history of Veuve Clicquot) was a booklet called *Wine in Peace and War* published by Saccone and Speed in 1947. It has never been reprinted, and has little of contemporary relevance in it. I observe from his correspondence with his agent, A.D. Peters, that he was paid at the rate of 12 bottles of champagne per 1000 words – not an immensely generous rate, I would say. Perhaps that explains why he wrote so little on the subject. I am sure he could have done better.

The last thing he wrote about wine appeared in the New York *Vogue* in the year before he died. It dealt with champagne, and described the circumstances in which it should be drunk: 'For two intimates, lovers or comrades, to spend a quiet evening with a magnum, drinking no apéritif before, nothing but a glass of cognac after – that is the ideal ... The worst time is that dictated by convention, in a crowd, in the early afternoon, at a wedding reception.'

That comment strikes me as profoundly true. Immense harm is done to champagne by the English habit of drinking it, usually warm and in a sort of trifle dish, at weddings in the early afternoon. That is why so many people in England claim to dislike champagne.

An even profounder claim is made in the first writing I have been able to trace by him in the December 1937 issue of *Harper's Bazaar*, under the title 'Laying Down a Wine Cellar.'

'Wine lives and dies; it has not only its hot youth, strong maturity and weary dotage, but also its seasonal changes, its mysterious, almost mystical, link with its parent vine, so that when the sap is running in the wood on the middle slopes of the Côte d'Or, in a thousand cellars a thousand miles away the wine in its bottle quickens and responds.'

I wonder if there is any truth in this theory. We have all noticed extraordinary variations from bottle to bottle within a matter of a month or two but I have never though of relating them to seasonal changes in Burgundy, Bordeaux, the Lebanon or wherever. Perhaps it is true that many wines – not ports nor old-fashioned 'cooked' Burgundies – go to sleep in the winter. If this is true, we should drink Australian, South African and Chilean wine throughout the winter, French wine only in the spring and summer months. California wines, by the same token, can be drunk all the year round.

Or perhaps it is all a load of codswallop. I was never entirely convinced that my father, for all his poetic gifts, knew very much about wine. Certainly his brother, Alec, knew much more. When Evelyn wrote those words, he was just laying down his first cellar. My grandfather, Arthur Waugh, who was a publisher and critic, drank nothing but Keystone Australian Burgundy, a beverage which he believed to have tonic properties, much to the embarrassment of his two sons.

Even so, my father, who wrote in 1937 that 'nothing is easier than to ruin a fine wine by careless handling,' was among the worst offenders in this respect. He never brought up a wine to the dining room more than half an hour before a meal – not that it would have made much difference if he had, as the dining room was nearly as cold as the cellar; and he never opened a bottle before it was time to drink it. In his last years he drank splendid burgundy, day after day, at temperatures which many would judge too cold for Sauternes.

But the saddest part of the article, written as a young man of 33, concerns ports of a great vintage; 'it is at least fifteen years before they become drinkable, and fifty before they are at their prime; some superlative vintages will live a century. It is these vintages which one should buy as soon as they are shipped and lay securely down for one's old age, or for posterity.'

Perhaps he had rather lost his enthusiasm for posterity by the time he died, at the sadly young age of 62. Despite his golden opportunity to lay down the 1963 vintage before his death in 1966, he left no port at all.

from *Number Three, St James's Street,*
House Magazine of Berry Bros. and Rudd, Spring 1986

The tragic fire which damaged *Le Coq Hardi* in 1995 caused serious damage to John's collection of wine. With resolute spirit he set about replac-
ing almost everything he lost. Some bottles with fire-damaged labels were bought
"on spec" at a sale at Adams of St Stephen's Green. Many people
bought "on spec", trusting that anything which
came from John Howard's cellar had to
be good. Very few were
disappointed.

6 An Honoured Guest

When a man is highly honoured and has
Eaten a little he is most benevolent.
                    Friedrich Nietzsche

The ideal number for a dinner party is two –
Myself and a dam' good head waiter.
                    Nubar Gulbenkian

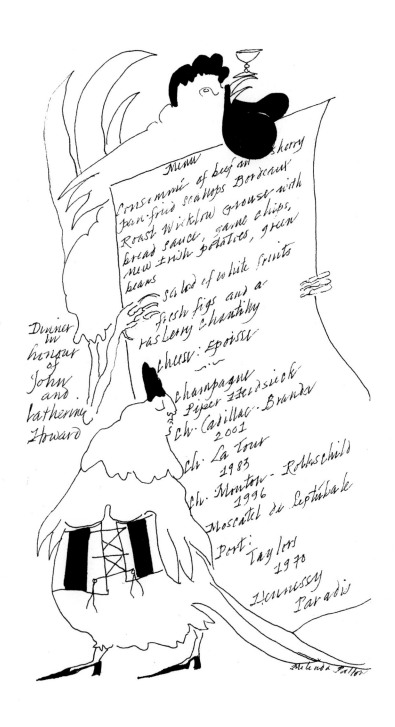

Menu

Consommé of beef and . . . . Sherry
Pan-fried scallops . . . . Bordeaux
Roast Wicklow Grouse with
bread sauce, game chips,
new Irish potatoes, green
beans

Salad of white fruits

Fresh figs and a
raspberry chantilly

Cheese: Epoisse

Dinner
in
honour
of
John
and
Katherine
Howard

Champagne
Piper Heidsieck
Ch. Cadillac-Branda
2001
Ch. La Tour
1983
Ch. Mouton-Rothschild
1996
Moscatel de Septibale

Port:
Taylors
1970

Hennessy
Paradis

Melinda Fallon

*T*o mark the completion of this book, the author asked a friend to devise a dinner entertainment for John and Catherine Howard. The request was for a classic dinner menu that even Mrs Beaton, if she were to take time out from her celestial kitchen, would find acceptable. Margaret Hyland, formerly of the Pembroke Restaurant, bravely took on the task of devising the menu and cooking the dinner for one of Ireland's most famous chefs. We reproduce her menu and recipes here. John Howard, being the perfect guest, gave it his unqualified approbation.

Menu

Consommé of Beef au Sherry
Pan-fried King Scallops Bordeaux Dressing
Roast Grouse with Bread Sauce, Game Chips, New Irish Potatoes and Green Beans
Salad of White Fruits in Champagne with Fresh Figs and a Raspberry Chantilly
Cheese: Epoisse

Wines

Champagne Piper-Heidsieck 1990
Château Cadillac-Branda 2001
Château Latour 1983
Château Mouton-Rothschild 1996
Moscatel de Setúbal
Dow's 1970
Hennessy Paradis

Recipes for the following dishes serve six persons:

Consommé

Ingredients

*Stock of shin beef for base with
    the following ingredients:*
1.5 kg of shin beef on the bone
0.5 kg rib of beef
2 l cold water
2 stalks of celery
2 medium carrots
Half a turnip
1 whole onion
2 bay leaves
Sprig each of thyme and parsley
4 eggs

Method

Brown all meats and drain off any residue of fat. Cover with water and vegetables and seasonings whole. Bring slowly to the boil. Separate whites of eggs and retain shells. Crush egg shell coarsely. Add to above and simmer gently for 4–5 hours. Strain through muslin and sieve. This reserved liquid is the basis of the consommé.

Ingredients for Consommé Proper

1 kg very finely chopped best quality beef
1 small carrot
1 stick celery
1 bay leaf
Pinch sea salt
Whole peppercorns

Method

- Add all of the above to the consommé base. Add water if required. Bring slowly to just under boiling point.

- Lightly whisk the egg whites. Pour on top while the mixture is still under boiling point. Leave to simmer for 2 hours. The egg whites clarify the consommé but it is vital not to allow the mixture to boil.

- Strain slowly through muslin. The result, though painstaking, should give a clear consommé. John Howard pronounced it, in particular, a triumph.

The lamp collector

The closing night

Finnegan
menton

17 Merrion Row, Dublin 2
Tel. 676 3914 Fax 678 5290
comm@finneganmenton.ie

For Sale By Tender Thursday 26th April 2001 (unless previously sold)

**Former Le Coq Hardi Restaurant
Internationally Renowned as one of Dublin's
finest Restaurants**

Former **"Le Coq Hardi"**
35 Pembroke Road, Dublin 4

**Total gross internal area:
422.2** sq.m./ **4,545** sq.ft.

**Superb Freehold
Commercial Premises
on corner of Wellington Road**

Solrs: Foley Solicitors, I Merrion Row, Dublin 2 Tel. 678 7879

Tel. 676 3914   Fax 678 5290

Pan Fried King Scallops Bordeaux Dressing

Ingredients

12 king scallops
25 g unsalted butter
Half a glass of good white Bordeaux
Watercress

Method

- On a hot pan melt the butter. For 40 seconds and 40 seconds only, let each side of the scallops see the pan.

- Remove scallops to a warm place on which a bed of cress has been settled. Pour wine on to the pan just long enough to warm it.

- Pour over the scallops and serve to table immediately.

Roast Grouse

Ingredients

150 g of butter
Juice of 1 lemon
6 young grouse
6 streaky rashers of bacon

Method

- Mix lemon and butter and rub all over the grouse, putting one teaspoon inside the grouse.

- Wrap each bird with a rasher of bacon.

- Place the birds individually in foil and secure. Roast in a pre-heated oven at Gas Mark 8, 200°C (425°F) for 45 minutes.

- Take the birds out of the fat, dredge with flour and brown the birds.

The last night at Le Coq Hardi

Bread Sauce

Ingredients

1 medium onion
4 cloves
0.5 l milk
25 g butter
50 ml cream
1 mace
50 g breadcrumbs
1 bay leaf

Method

- Simmer the milk.

- Place the cloves in the onion and to the milk, then add the bay leaf and the mace.

- Simmer again until the onion is soft. Leave to cool and infuse.

- Strain the liquid. Stir in the breadcrumbs, butter and cream. Stir until thickened.

Game Chips

Ingredients

6 rooster potatoes
Vegetable oil for deep frying

Method

- Slice potatoes paper thin leaving the skin on.

- Run under cold water until all the starch has vanished. Dry them in a paper towel until all are completely dry.

- Plunge into hot oil a handful at a time for approximately 1 minute. Drain on paper towel. Serve hot.

The final toast – left to right, Darren Campbell, José Martinhoe,
Nicholas Allas and Michael Birch

Salad of White Fruits

Ingredients

3 pears
3 apples
0.5 kg of white seedless grapes
Dash of Maraschino
1 glass Champagne

Method

- Peel all the fruit, including grapes. Cut into small pieces. Cover with champagne and good dash of Maraschino.
- Leave overnight in fridge.
- Serve chilled.

Figs Chantilly

30 fresh ripe figs
6 punnets of raspberries
0.5 l double cream
100 g vanilla sugar

Method

⟐ Peel figs and quarter them. Place in shallow bowl. Whip cream and sugar until firm. Fold in sieved raspberries and cover figs. Chill for 3–4 hours.

NOTE FROM MISS HYLAND: This elaborate dinner took two days and infinite patience to prepare. It is not for the faint-hearted. Stay calm and have a decent drink to hand at all times!

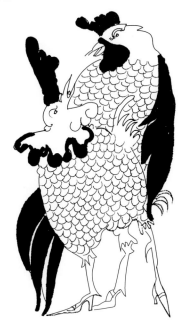

The final curtain

Scholastic Literacy Skills

C000202016

VOCABULARY

Term-by-Term Photocopiables

ERNEHALE JUNIOR SCHOOL
Derwent Crescent
Arnold
Nottinghamshire
NG5 6TA
Tel: 0115 956 8008 Fax: 0115 956 8006

AUTHORS CLAIRE COLLING, VAL GREEN,
CHRIS HOLLOWAY AND SALLY JOHNSON
EDITOR CLARE GALLAHER
ASSISTANT EDITOR ROANNE DAVIS
SERIES DESIGNER MARK UDALL
DESIGNER RACHAEL HAMMOND
ILLUSTRATIONS TONY O'DONNELL

Designed using Adobe Pagemaker
Published by Scholastic Ltd, Villiers House, Clarendon Avenue,
Leamington Spa, Warwickshire CV32 5PR
Text © Claire Colling, Val Green,
Chris Holloway and Sally Johnson
© 2000 Scholastic Ltd
1 2 3 4 5 6 7 8 9 0   0 1 2 3 4 5 6 7 8
British Library Cataloguing-in-Publication Data
A catalogue record for this book is available
from the British Library.
ISBN 0-439-01642-8

The right of Claire Colling, Val Green, Chris Holloway
and Sally Johnson to be identified as the Authors of this
Work has been asserted by them in accordance with the
Copyright, Designs and Patents Act 1988.

All rights reserved. This book is sold subject to the
condition that it shall not, by way of trade or otherwise,
be lent, hired out or otherwise circulated without the
publisher's prior consent in any form of binding or cover
other than that in which it is published and without a
similar condition, including this condition, being
imposed upon the subsequent purchaser.

No part of this publication may be reproduced, stored in a
retrieval system, or transmitted, in any form or by any
means, electronic, mechanical, photocopying, recording
or otherwise, without the prior permission of the
publisher. This book remains copyright, although
permission is granted to copy pages where indicated, for
classroom distribution and use only in the school which
has purchased the book, or by the teacher who has
purchased this book and in accordance with the CLA
licensing agreement. Photocopying permission is given
for purchasers only and not for borrowers of books from
any lending service.

Contents

vocabulary

Vocabulary

The four books in this series are designed to develop children's vocabulary skills through progressive worksheets that are structured to fit the school year.

Written by practising teachers, the content emphasizes the development of vocabulary and spelling based on the word and sentence level requirements of the National Literacy Strategy *Framework for Teaching*.

The photocopiable worksheets in each book give opportunities for pupils to work independently of the teacher to enhance their word power. Alternatively, teachers may wish to use the sheets as a focus for whole-class shared teaching or for homework.

Themes

Each *Vocabulary* book is loosely arranged on a theme of 'exploration'. This reinforces the idea that children, by exploring and being curious about words, will develop strategies for further increasing their word power. The themes for each book are:

- ❏ ages 7–8: Jungle explorer
- ❏ ages 8–9: Underwater explorer
- ❏ ages 9–10: Underground explorer
- ❏ ages 10–11: Space explorer

Word Explorer

Each *Vocabulary* book contains a photocopiable Word Explorer booklet which matches the theme of the book. The Word Explorer encourages each child to collect new words and learn new meanings by building a personal wordbank. For example, the children may have one sheet on which they write down new words as indicated by the Word Explorer magnifying glass symbol shown on the worksheets. In addition, teachers may choose themes or sets of words related to a topic or particular theme being covered at the time, for example words related to a topic on the Greeks, or a science theme such as 'photosynthesis'.

Treasure Tests

The Treasure Test words are target words that children should learn. There are six pages of these in each book, two for each term, which children can take home to learn (see pages 9, 10, 26, 27, 44 and 45). They can test their knowledge of Treasure Test words at the end of each term with the Treasure Chest sheet on page 64. Teachers may choose to use this as an assessment guide in the form of a test or, alternatively, children of similar ability could test each other to reinforce their knowledge.

The Treasure Tests are progressive and consolidatory – that is, the word lists for ages 8–9 revise and consolidate vocabulary from the ages 7–8 *Vocabulary* book, and so on. The children may wish to keep the Treasure Test sheets and Word Explorer booklets in their own personal folders or portfolios.

Answers

These are given on pages 4–6. Some activities are open-ended and, where appropriate, suggestions are provided.

Guide to symbols used

 = magnifying glass. This denotes new or challenging words which should be added to the Word Explorer booklet.

 = dictionary/thesaurus. This symbol indicates children will need to use a dictionary and/or thesaurus to complete the task.

 = Treasure Chest. The Treasure Chest symbol denotes more challenging tasks which may be suitable for extension work.

Answers

Plot the stars (page 11)

Possible answers: recede, receded, receding, recedes, concede, conceded, conceding, concedes, conclude, concluded, concluding, concludes, include, included, including, includes, exclude, excluded, excluding, excludes, concept, conception, concepts, except, exception, report, reported, reporting, reports, deport, deported, deporting, deports, export, exported, exporting, exports, import, importance, imported, importing, imports, reappear, reappearance, reappeared, reappearing, reappears, disappear, disappeared, disappearing, disappears, describe, describable, described, describing, describes, inscribe, inscribed, inscribes, depart, departed, departing, departs, impart, imparted, imparting, imparts, portable, portion, ports, appearance, appeared, appearing, scribes, parted, parting, parts.

Aero (page 12)

Possible words: aerobatics, aerobics, aerobiology, aerodrome, aerodynamics, aerofoil, aerogram, aerolite, aerology, aerometer, aerometry, aeronaut, aerophobia, aerophone, aerophyte, aeroplane, aerosol, aerospace, aerostat, aerotrain. Aero = having to do with air or aircraft.

Suffixes in space! (page 13)

teleport, import, export, airport, deport; include, preclude, conclude; subscribe, inscribe, prescribe, describe; precede, recede; telescope.

Spot the suffix (page 14)

Answer should be similar to: a morpheme added at the end of a group of letters to make a new word.
prescribe; import; precede; subscribe; include; recede; export; preclude.
1. import; 2. subscribe; 3. include; 4. recede; 5. precede; 6. prescribe; 7. export; 8. preclude.

Connectives in space (page 15)

Having; Therefore; until; Nevertheless; Furthermore/Therefore.

From simple to complex (page 16)

1. but, and/so; 2. who, after; 3. As soon as/When/After/Because, which.

Journey to the Moon (page 17)

thou: you; goest: goes; thy: your; hath: have; doeth: do; thee: you; alack: an expression of regret or surprise, for example 'Oh no!'; pantry: storeroom/larder; yonder: over there or in that direction; verily: truly; behold: see or observe; shalt: shall; thence: from that place; whence: (to the place) from which; cometh: comes; thine: your; hither: to/towards this place; victuals: food; whither: 1) to what place, position or state or 2) to which; abide: remain/continue or dwell/live; roving: wandering; saeth: says.
1. Truly/honestly I tell you; 2. What are you thinking? or What do you think?; 3. Where are you going?; 4. friends and relations.

Dictionary explorer (page 18)

The dictionary definitions are: fly-drive: a holiday which includes the cost of car rental along with the flight; sleazeball: horrible, unpleasant person; rollerblade: a boot fitted underneath with a line of small wheels, for gliding on smooth surfaces; ram-raid: a robbery in which a shop window is smashed by a vehicle and the contents of the shop are stolen; qwerty: the name for the standard English language keyboard (taken from the top line of keys); all-star: teams or groups made up wholly of high-quality, famous performers; wheelie: riding a bicycle or motorbike with the front wheel raised from the ground; snowboarding: using one wider ski for gliding on snow; Internet: international computer network linking many organizations; compact disc: a disc on which information or sound is recorded digitally and reproduced by the reflection of laser light.

Origins of names 1 (page 19)

Janus – January; Augustus – August; Mars – March; Tiw – Tuesday; Woden – Wednesday; Thor – Thursday; Frig – Friday; Saturn – Saturday.

Origins of names 2 (page 20)

Examples are: 1. Manchester, Chesterfield, Lancaster, Leicester; 2. Portsmouth, Bridport, Southport; 3. Streetly, Street, Stratford; 4. Tonbridge, Nuneaton, Warrington; 5. Hampstead, Birmingham, Nottingham; 6. Doncaster, London, Swindon; 7. Middlesborough, Edinburgh, Newbury. Occupation: Baker, Smith, Fletcher, Shepherd, Mason, Archer, Thatcher; Habitat: Hill, Field, Meadows, Brook, Forest.

'et' go home (page 21)

Derived from a place or person: wellington, cardigan, sandwich, balaclava; Loan word from a different country: restaurant, café, anorak, bungalow; Derived from a Latin or Greek root: telegraph, automatic, democracy, biology.

To go boldly (page 22)

beside; Nearby; between; Firstly; secondly; finally; As; because; upon; since; beneath; Wherever; as; across; even if; As long as; although; whether; or.

The aliens are here! (page 23)

commander; tall; striking; grouped; similar; visible; concealed; bronze/silver; slanting; protruding; gazed; fearfully; friendly/hostile; hostile/friendly; encased; suit; gloved; waist; gleaming; silver/bronze; shoulders; cape; broad; chest; symbolizing; crescent; moon; brilliantly; disbelieving.

Can you remember? (page 24)

Children's own answers.

Space sense (page 25)

1. A strong force called gravity tries to pull the rocket back down; 2. A rocket has to have an engine powerful enough to launch a spacecraft into space; 3. It is the second stage rocket that takes the spacecraft into orbit.
4. An astronaut made a space walk from Gemini 4 in 1965.
5. When Gemini returned it used parachutes to help it splash down into the sea.

Look before you leap (page 28)

Answers should be similar to: 1. Do not rely on success before the matter is concluded; 2. Two minds solving a problem are better than one; 3. Do not stir up trouble unnecessarily; 4. While the threat of punishment is absent unruly behaviour may result; 5. The sooner a task is tackled the greater is the chance of success; 6. If there are too many people involved in a task, disaster may result.

More proverbs (page 29)

Proverb numbers, in order: 4, 7, 5, 1, 6, 8, 2, 3.

Flight (page 30)

space; adaptations; Crete; undone; unfurled; height; home; destruction; stars; race; speed; ground.
contraptions, adaptations; Greeks, Crete; unknown, home.

Space chain (page 31)

Answers should be similar to: Across: 1. a container for astronauts or scientific instruments which can be sent into space and recovered when it returns; 3. the study of planets and stars; 6. of the Moon; 7. a person who studies science in depth; 9. a rocky body which burns up as it falls through

Earth's atmosphere; 11. the passing of one planet or satellite in front of another causing a loss of light; 14. a small rocky body orbiting the Sun; 18. a star which suddenly becomes much brighter and then fades again; 19. a large hole or depression in the surface of the Earth, Moon and so on; 20. the planet in the solar system where we live.
Down: 2. a space traveller; 4. the planet fourth in order from the Sun; 5. a body which revolves around another, an artificial body sent into orbit by man; 8. a reusable rocket-propelled craft which can carry equipment between Earth and a satellite; 10. moved round in a curved path; 12. a celestial body of rock and ice which moves around the Sun and which seems to have a tail; 13. protective clothing worn by an astronaut; 15. a curved path made by a satellite or planet around a larger body; 16. a large system of stars and planets; 17. a force of attraction which pulls small bodies to Earth.

Journey into space (page 32)

-ible (in any order): invisible, impossible, reversible, responsible, possible, terrible, incredible, sensible, flexible, edible.
-able (in any order): probable, valuable, lovable, comfortable, drinkable, capable, suitable, remarkable, reasonable, fashionable, reliable, noticeable.

Cut it short (page 33)

Answer should be similar to: 1. The solar system is believed to have been created 4600 million years ago; 2. The Sun, the nearest star to Earth, is at the centre of the solar system; 3. There are nine planets that orbit the Sun in the same direction with oval paths; 4. The nine planets which differ in size are called Mercury, Venus, Earth, Mars, Jupiter, Saturn, Uranus, Neptune and Pluto.
Planets in order: 1. Mercury, 2. Venus, 3. Earth, 4. Mars, 5. Jupiter, 6. Saturn, 7. Uranus, 8. Neptune, 9. Pluto.

Key words and bullet points (page 34)

plants; sequoias; grow; twigs; branches; wood; bark; roots; trunk; stem; tubes; leaves; chlorophyll; deciduous; evergreen.
Answer should be similar to:
• Trees are the largest plants on Earth.
• They continue to grow in all directions throughout their lives.
• Roots supply trees with water and nutrients; they anchor trees in the soil.
• The stem of the tree, the trunk, pumps water from the roots to all other parts of the tree.
• Branches and twigs support the leaves.
• Leaves make food by capturing sunlight energy.
• The green substance in plants is called chlorophyll.
• There are two types of tree, deciduous and evergreen.
• Deciduous trees lose their leaves every autumn and evergreen trees keep theirs for a number of years.

The first spacewoman (page 35)

1937 – Tereshkova born; 1959 – first parachute jump; 1962 – begins cosmonaut training; 1963 – chosen for crew of Vostok 6; 1964 – daughter, Alyonka, born; 1977 – awarded UN Gold Medal of Peace.

Know your books (page 36)

Across: 4. encyclopedia; 6. dictionary; 9. glossary; 12. publisher; 14. title; 16. editor; 17. date; 19. surname; 20. magazine; 21. directory.
Down: 1. thesaurus; 2. atlas; 3. newspaper; 5. index; 7. alphabetical; 8. bibliography; 10. yellow; 11. contents; 13. reference; 15. illustrator; 18. author.

Let's get active (page 37)

1. Our spacecraft was carrying much information about life on Earth; 2. Four of the crew guarded this cargo carefully at all times; 3. As we landed, Commander Crontag, leader of

Planet Splontia, welcomed us; 4. The Splontians fed the information that we gave them into their computer database; 5. The Splontians gave us specimens of plant life to study back on Earth; 6. A giant meteor hit the rocket; 7. We orbited Venus for three days; 8. Ground Control gave me the go-ahead to land.

Pegasus and Andromeda (page 38)

Suggestions for other words (in order): fine; good; clear; bright; magnificent; interesting; beautiful; sparkling; exciting; brave; glittering; brilliant.

Anagrams (page 39)

1. almost; 2. birthday; 3. clothes; 4. different; 5. earth; 6. father; 7. friend; 8. garden; 9. half; 10. important; 11. jumped; 12. know; 13. light; 14. money; 15. number.

Space puzzles (page 40)

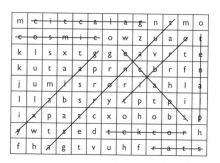

Answers should be similar to: Across: 2. a group of stars; 5. the planet we live on; 7. relating to the Sun; 8. relating to the Moon; 10. the area outside the Earth's atmosphere.
Down: 1. one celestial body passing in front of another causing darkness; 3. a being from another planet; 4. the eighth planet from the Sun; 6. Saturn's largest satellite; 9. an engine which can be used to launch spacecrafts.

The phases of the Moon (page 41)

diferent – different; chainges – changes; beggin – begin; folowed – followed; rownd – round; lite – light; Erth – Earth; beetween – between; upun – upon; yeer – year.

Now and then (page 42)

Suggested answers: web: this can refer to a web page or the world wide web (made up of websites); boot: start up/make ready; mouse: small, hand-held device for operating a computer; surf: search subjects on the Internet, visiting websites; keyboard; set of keys to control, and input information into, a computer; disk: computer data storage device; program: set of coded instructions used by a computer; to log: to input personal information to access a computer's programs; monitor: unit that displays computer data; screen: the surface of a monitor on which images appear.
web: spider's construction for trapping prey, membrane between toes of ducks, frogs and so on; boot: a kind of footwear, storage compartment at the rear of a car; mouse: a small rodent; surf: foam and swell of the sea; keyboard; a set of keys on a musical instrument, for example a piano; disc/disk: a thin circular plate of any material, a thin layer of cartilage between vertebrae; program(me): a printed list of a series of events at a performance; to log: make a systematic record of events (for example, a ship's log); monitor: a pupil with special responsibilities designated by the teacher; screen: a fixed or movable partition.

Alien argument (page 43)

Children write their own arguments.

What's your phobia? (page 46)

2. agoraphobia – fear of open spaces or public places; 3. acrophobia – fear of high places; 4. hydrophobia – fear of

water; 5. xenophobia – fear of strangers or foreigners;
6. claustrophobia – fear of enclosed places.

Dictionary delving (page 47)

1. alien; 2. asteroid; 3. astronaut; 4. astronomical;
5. astronomy; 6. atmosphere.
1. galactic; 2. galaxy; 3. gas; 4. geology; 5. global; 6. globe.
Suggestions: 2 letters: at, in, it, on, no, so, to; 3 letters: ale,
all, ate, con, cot, eat, let, net, not, sat, set, son, tan, ten, tie,
tin; 4 letters: call, cone, lane, last, late, lean, lice, lint, lion,
list, loan, lone, lose, lost, nail, neat, nest, nice, nose, note,
sail, sale, salt, sane, scan, seal, sell, sent, soil, sole, tail, tale,
tall, tell, tent, tile, toll, tone; 5 letters: alien, alone, atone,
coast, lance, leant, least, noise, saint, salon, scale, scent,
scone, slant, slate, slice, stain, stale, stall, state, steal, stile,
stole, stone, taint, talon, taste, toast, tonal, total; 6 letters:
action, latent, latest, lotion, nation, notice, notion, solace,
stance, static, talent; 7 letters or more: console, constant,
contest, elastic, elation, install, instance, stallion, station.

A nebula of nouns (page 48)

Common nouns: crater, star, eclipse, orbit, shuttle, comet,
satellite, rocket, meteor, astronaut, asteroid.
Proper nouns: Venus, Uranus, Pegasus, Great Bear, Pluto,
Milky Way, Orion, Polaris, Neil Armstrong, Galileo, Jupiter,
Halley's Comet, the Plough.
Abstract nouns: gravity, eternity, universe, weightlessness.
Collective nouns: constellation, galaxy, cluster.

Black hole! (page 49)

Possible answers: unlike, unlikely, unlikeable, unacceptable,
depend, dependable, dependent, dependant, dislike, disappear,
disappearance, disappoint, impossible, invisible, improbable,
acceptance, acceptable, appointment, appointable, probable,
visible, appearance, possible, likeable, likely.

Alien astronaut (page 50)

Thursday; day; care; fear; trepidation; authorization; take-
off; sensations; countdown; mixture; emotions; excitement;
curiosity; anxiety; joy; life; sigh; relief; while; destination.
frightened – fear/fright; excited – excitement; apprehensive –
apprehension; content – contentment; courageous – courage;
brave – bravery; impatient – impatience; hopeful – hope.

A galaxy of stars (page 51)

1. army/troop; 2. orchestra/band; 3. crew; 4. herd; 5. flock;
6. band/gang; 7. herd; 8. litter; 9. pack; 10. swarm.
1. bouquet/bunch; 2. chest; 3. flight; 4. hedge; 5. library;
6. pack; 7. string/rope; 8. wardrobe/suit; 9. bunch/hand;
10. peal.
Suggested answers (many others are possible): 1. wild
animals; 2. people; 3. soldiers; 4. sticks; 5. leaves; 6. eggs;
7. shoes; 8. guns; 9. pencils; 10. people.

Glimmering limericks (page 52)

Mars; space.

Shooting stars (page 53)

1. wine and dine; 2. dream team; 3. hotpot; 4. hogwash;
5. horses for courses; 6. country bumpkin; 7. scallywag;
8. hither and thither; 9. hocus-pocus; 10. hanky-panky;
11. hot dog; 12. shop 'til you drop; 13. flapjack; 14. mean
machine; 15. willy-nilly; 16. hotchpotch; 17. hoity-toity; 18.
high-flyer; 19. roller-coaster; 20. flower power.

The alien plant (page 54)

Children choose their own words to rewrite the passage.

Fact or fiction (page 55)

1. fact; 2. fiction; 3. fiction; 4. fiction; 5. fact; 6. fiction;
7. fact; 8. fact; 9. fiction; 10. fact; 11. fact; 12. fact; 13.
fiction; 14. fact; 15. fiction.

Don't say that again! (page 56)

1. fatally injured, died: The driver was fatally injured/The
driver died.
2. annual, every year: The Christmas fair is held every year
in the town hall/The Christmas fair in the town hall is an
annual event.
3. foreigner, from another country: The person came from
another country/The person was a foreigner.
4. baby, foal: The foal trotted beside its mother.
5. Lined up one after another, in the queue: The people in
the queue were served in the post office/One after another,
the people were served in the post office.
6. cargo, being carried on board: The cargo on the ship was
mainly sugar/The ship's cargo was mainly sugar.
7. raw, uncooked: The meat couldn't be eaten because it was
raw/uncooked.
8. bungalow, built on one storey: The bungalow was a pretty
house.
9. looked crossly, glared: The driver looked crossly/glared at
the dent in his bumper.
10. Nobody knew, anonymous: Nobody knew who had
written the poem.

Into the future (page 57)

I will fly over 400,000 miles. I will journey through space,
faster than the speed of light. I will travel towards a new
planet and will look forward to finding new life there. As I
get closer to the planet, I will check my controls to ensure
the planet can sustain life. I will flick the control switch and
send a message back to base to confirm my estimated time
of touchdown. I will switch the controls to landing mode
and approach the planet's surface with caution – and will
wonder what awaits me.

Moony metaphors (page 58)

The aliens were little, rubbery blobs of a jelly-like substance.
Our companion spaceship was a silver spinning top
hovering far above.
Huge craters opened their great, yawning mouths on the
dark landscape.
Dark mountains pointed their cold, eerie fingers upwards.
A far-off planet was a glittering, crystal ball.
The screen was a kaleidoscope of magical colours and forms.

Word games (page 59)

Suggested answers: 2 moves: cup – cut – but; rip – sip – sit;
3 moves: race – pace – pale – palm; slow – glow – grow –
brow; 4 moves: farm – harm – harp – carp – camp; head –
heat – peat – pear – fear.
1. ozone; 2. temperature; 3. telescope; 4. expedition;
5. vapour; 6. meteorite.

Words within words (page 60)

The prefix *tele* means 'at a distance'.

Abbreviations and acronyms (page 61)

Royal Automobile Club; United Nations; very high
frequency; Football Association; do-it-yourself; Amateur
Athletics Association.
Royal Society for the Protection of Birds; Los Angeles; United
States of America; as soon as possible; stamped addressed
envelope; Royal Society for the Prevention of Cruelty to
Animals; for the attention of; postscript; Financial Times;
very important person.

So, you want to be an astronaut (page 62)

Possible answers are that astronauts should be: 1, 3, 4, 7, 8,
13, 14, 18 and 20.

A safe landing (page 63)

Children write their own descriptions.

Name _____

Class _____

School address _____
_____
_____
_____

Word Explorer

Design your own colour key.

vocabulary

photocopiable

Write any new words you have learned.

☐

Treasure Test 1

❏ Can you spell these words on your empty Treasure Chest sheet? Ask a friend to test you on them. Remember! Look, say, cover, write, check.
Write down each word three times. Every time you get it right, colour in a star in the rocket on the Treasure Chest sheet.

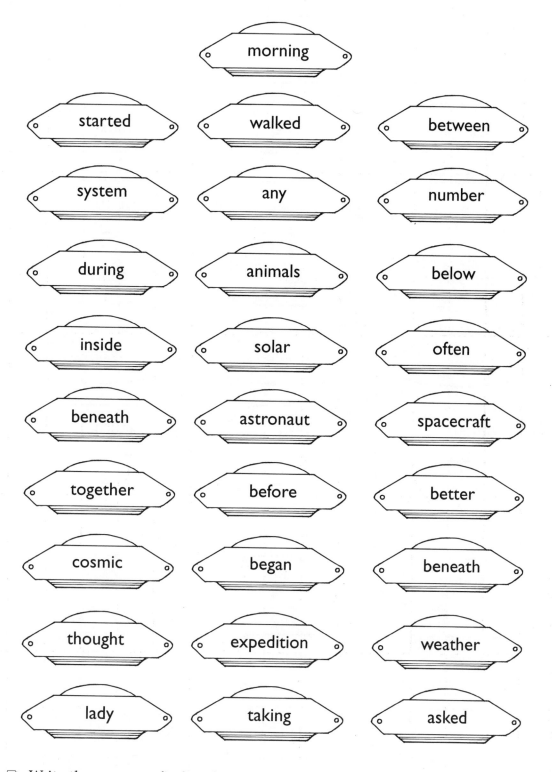

 ❏ Write the ones you find tricky in your Word Explorer.

Treasure Test 2

❑ Can you spell these words on your empty Treasure Chest sheet? Ask a friend to test you on them. Remember! Look, say, cover, write, check.

Write down each word three times. Every time you get it right, colour in a star in the rocket on the Treasure Chest sheet.

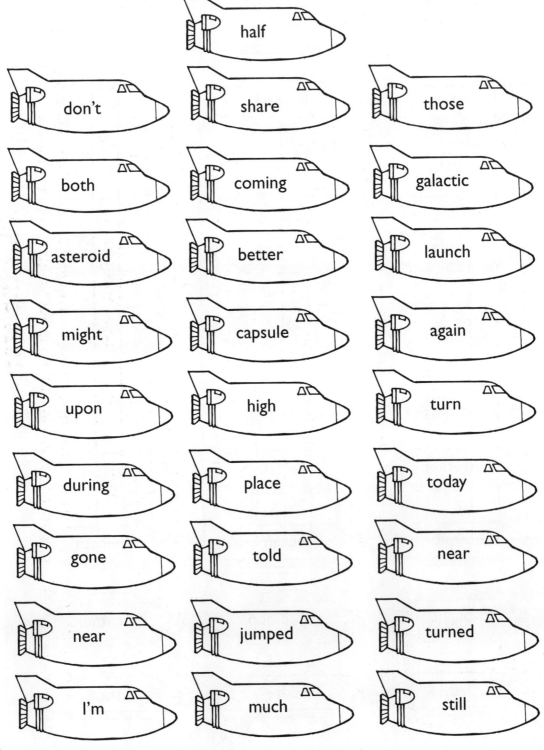

half

don't   share   those

both   coming   galactic

asteroid   better   launch

might   capsule   again

upon   high   turn

during   place   today

gone   told   near

near   jumped   turned

I'm   much   still

❑ Write the ones you find tricky in your Word Explorer.

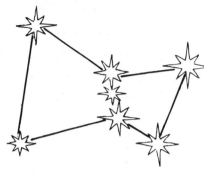

Plot the stars

❑ As an astronomer searches the skies for star constellations, search the grid for words. You can join a prefix to a root word or add a suffix to a root word. You might find you can join all three columns. Write your answers in the box below the grid.

Prefix	Root word	Suffix
re	cede	able
con	clude	ance
de	cept	ed
in	cred	ing
dis	port	ion
ex	appear	ive
un	scribe	s
im	part	tion

Words found

Orion

Pole Star

Plough

Southern Cross

photocopiable

Aero

❏ Use your dictionary to find words with the prefix **aero**.
Make a glossary of the words. Don't forget to write them
in alphabetical order.

Glossary work	
Word	**Definition**

❏ From your work, what do you think the prefix **aero** means?

_____

Suffixes in space!

A suffix is added to the end of a group of letters to make a new word.

(teleport)   (airport)   **port** is the suffix.

❏ Match the suffixes in the rockets to the letters in each planet:

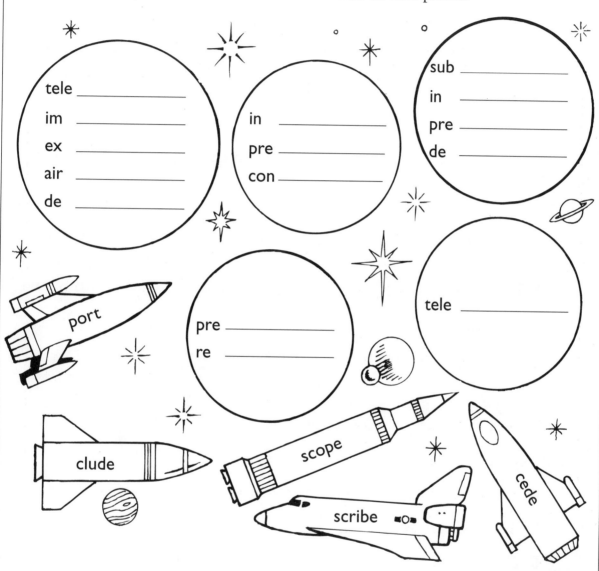

❏ Use your dictionary to find the definitions of five of the words you have made.
Write five sentences, each of which uses one of the words.

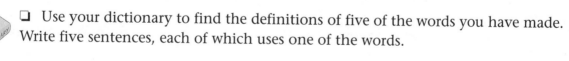

1 _____

2 _____

3 _____

4 _____

5 _____

Spot the suffix

What is a suffix? _____

❏ Underline the suffix in each of these words:

prescribe   import   precede

subscribe   include   recede

export   preclude

❏ Now choose the correct word to complete each sentence:

1 The company will _____ the exotic fruits into Britain
next week.

2 She enjoyed reading the magazine and has decided to _____
to it.

3 When he sent the letter to his pen-pal, he forgot to _____
a photo of himself.

4 James was sixty years old and as well as his face having more wrinkles
his hair had started to _____ .

5 The magician's act will _____ the singer on the
programme because the names will be in alphabetical order.

6 If you are ill, the doctor may _____ some medication
for you.

7 I am hoping to _____ the goods abroad.

8 The fact that Thomas is related to the defendant in the case will
_____ him from being a member of the jury.

Connectives in space

nevertheless

until

furthermore

therefore

having

❏ Choose the most suitable connective from those on the rockets to complete this diary extract:

Commander's Log: Date 25.9.3589

_____ checked over my Galactic Transporter, I was dissatisfied with the condition of the teleportation unit. _____ I ordered the crew to disembark _____ all systems had been thoroughly inspected by the chief engineer. _____ the journey to Planet Zintag went ahead on schedule. _____ ,we arrived in time to view the eclipse of Zintag's moon.

❏ Complete these sentences about what you did at break:

1 It was raining heavily at breaktime, therefore I _____
_____
_____

2 Notwithstanding the heavy rainfall that had occurred, at breaktime I
_____
_____

3 It was raining at breaktime, nevertheless I _____
_____
_____

4 It had rained continually overnight and throughout the morning.
Furthermore _____
_____

From simple to complex

A complex sentence is one that is longer and more interesting than a simple sentence. Conjunctions and connectives are often used to link a number of simple sentences together to make a more complex one.

> *Simple sentences:* She went to the shop. She bought some sweets. They were her favourites.
> *Complex sentence:* She went to the shop **where** she bought some sweets **which** were her favourites.

❏ Make these simple sentences into complex ones by using suitable connectives or conjunctions from the box below. Use each one only once.

1 I love skiing. My sister doesn't. She refuses to come with me.

I love skiing, _____ my sister doesn't _____ she refuses to come with me.

2 Yesterday I visited my aunt. She has become ill with influenza. She had been for a walk in the rain.

Yesterday I visited my aunt _____ has become ill with influenza _____ having been for a walk in the rain.

3 I had finished reading my book. It was interesting. I asked to go to the library.

_____ I had finished reading my book, _____ was interesting, I asked to go to the library.

> as soon as, if, therefore, because, which, although, when, now that, while, before, after, and, however, so, so that, who, but, where

❏ Make these simple sentences into complex ones by adding more detail to them. Use *different* connectives or conjunctions from the ones you have used above. Write them on a separate sheet.

1 I finished my story.
2 On Saturday we went shopping in the city.
3 Yesterday it was raining so heavily.
4 Pasta is my favourite food.
5 We will be able to go on holiday.

Journey to the Moon

In the past, people tried unsuccessfully to build towers to get to the Moon. As scientific knowledge has developed, we can now travel there.
Over the years, many new words have been added to our language and quite a few have fallen out of use.

Welcome to the Moon!

❏ Can you find modern-day versions of these very old words? Write them in the spaces on the tower.

thou _____

goest _____

thy _____

hath _____

doeth _____

thee _____

alack _____

pantry _____

yonder _____

verily _____

behold _____

shalt _____

thence _____

whence _____

cometh _____

thine _____

hither _____

victuals _____

whither _____

abide _____

roving _____

saeth _____

Hello up there!

To the Moon

❏ Write the modern-day versions of these phrases:

1 Verily, I sayeth unto you.

_____

2 What thinkest thou?

_____

3 Whither thou goest?

_____

4 kith and kin

_____

Dictionary explorer

New words are continually finding their way into our vocabulary and being added to our dictionaries.
The words below appear in a 1990s dictionary but not in a 1980 dictionary.

❑ On line (a) write your own definitions of the word.
❑ On line (b) write the dictionary definition. Make sure you use an up-to-date dictionary!

fly-drive   (a) _____

                   (b) _____

sleazeball   (a) _____

                   (b) _____

rollerblade   (a) _____

                   (b) _____

ram-raid   (a) _____

                   (b) _____

querty   (a) _____

                   (b) _____

all-star   (a) _____

                   (b) _____

wheelie   (a) _____

                   (b) _____

snowboarding   (a) _____

                   (b) _____

Internet   (a) _____

                   (b) _____

compact disc   (a) _____

                   (b) _____

❑ Can you find more words which have recently been added to the dictionary?

photocopiable

Origins of names 1

Many of the names of days of the week and months of the year come from the names of gods and goddesses or famous leaders of the past.

❑ Look at the descriptions in the clouds and 'map' them to the correct days of the week or months of the year. One has been done for you.

❑ Look in dictionaries and encyclopedias to find information about the origins of the names.

Julius Caesar, famous Roman Emperor

Tuesday

Wednesday

Saturn, Roman god of agriculture

Tiw, Norse god of the sky and of war

Woden, chief god in Anglo-Saxon mythology

January

July

Saturday

Thursday

Augustus, Roman Emperor

Thor, Norse god of thunder, rain and farming

March

August

Janus, Roman god of doorways and beginnings, shown with two faces

Friday

Frig, Norse goddess of clouds, sky and love

Mars, Roman god of war

Origins of names 2

If you want to find out about the village, town or city in which you live, you can research the origin of its name in a dictionary of place-names. Here are some common parts of place-names and their meanings:

1 **-chester**, **Chester-**, **-caster**, **-cester**   Roman fort or town
2 **Port-**, **-port**   harbour or town with walls and a gate
3 **Street-**, **-street**, **Strat-**   on a Roman road
4 **Ton-**, **-ton**   old English farm or manor
5 **Ham-**, **-ham**   meadow or homestead
6 **Don-**, **-don**   down, meaning 'hill'
7 **-borough**, **-burgh**, **-bury**   fortified camp, house or hill-fort

❏ Use a map of Britain to find three place-names in each category above:

1 _____ _____ _____
2 _____ _____ _____
3 _____ _____ _____
4 _____ _____ _____
5 _____ _____ _____
6 _____ _____ _____
7 _____ _____ _____

Some surnames show their origins in the occupations or habitats of people.
❏ Place the surnames in this list into the correct columns:

Baker,   Smith,   Hill,   Fletcher,   Field,   Shepherd,   Meadows,
Mason,   Brook,   Archer,   Thatcher,   Forest

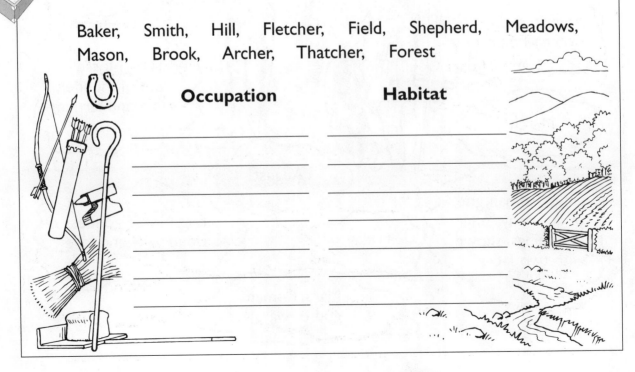

Occupation	Habitat
_____	_____
_____	_____
_____	_____
_____	_____
_____	_____

'et' go home

Etymology is the investigation of the origins of words.

❑ Find the origins of the words on the asteroids and send them home by writing them on the correct planet.

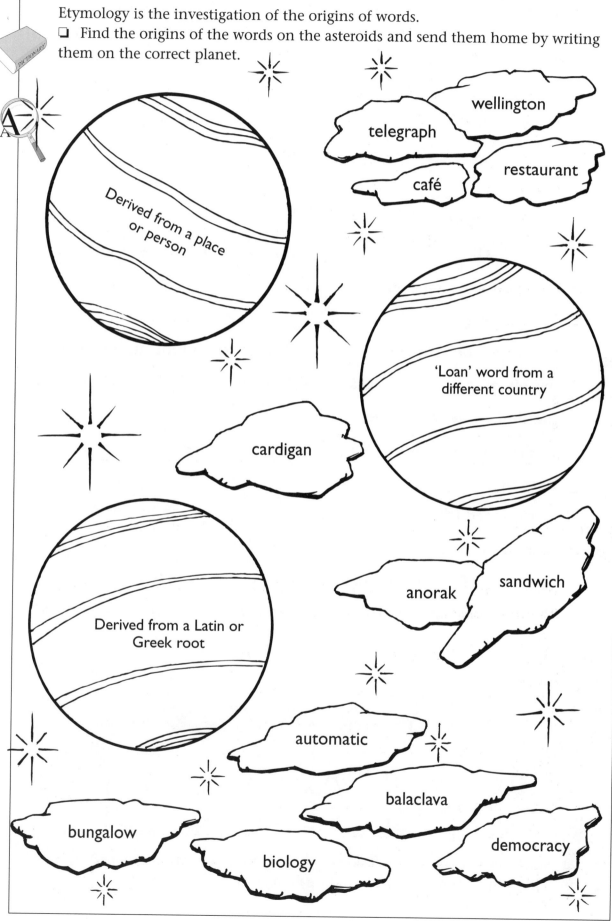

wellington

telegraph

café

restaurant

Derived from a place or person

'Loan' word from a different country

cardigan

anorak

sandwich

Derived from a Latin or Greek root

automatic

balaclava

bungalow

biology

democracy

photocopiable

To go boldly

In this passage there are two groups of connectives within each pair of brackets. One of the group of connectives is the correct one to select so that the passage makes sense.

❑ Underline the correct connectives.

The spacecraft landed (**underneath, beside**) a low crater. (**About, Nearby**) were dry valleys running (**between, along**) jagged mountains.

(**Firstly, lastly**) I found my life-support suit, (**because, secondly**) I put on my breathing apparatus and (**finally, until**) I walked gingerly towards the opening door onto a new world.

(**Because, As**) I left the craft I felt a mixture of excitement and fear (**although, because**) I was the first human to set foot (**upon, inside**) this planet. It was two weeks (**now that, since**) I had felt solid ground (**behind, beneath**) my feet.

(**Whenever, Wherever**) I gazed, my eyes settled upon a harsh rocky landscape.

Frightened (**through, as**) I was, I staggered (**across, against**) the dusty uneven surface. I could not turn back (**even if, except that**) I wanted to. (**As long as, As though**) I had radio contact with Earth, I had the confidence to proceed, (**whenever, although**) I must confess that I wasn't certain (**whether, since**) I would return home safely (**or, as**) not.

❑ Bring this story to its conclusion. You might want to write collaboratively (with a partner). How can you introduce more characters?

The aliens are here!

commander
disbelieving
similar
visible
concealed
symbolizing
fearfully
moon
bronze
brilliantly
broad

protruding
encased
friendly
hostile
striking
gazed
silver
suit
cape
crescent
tall
slanting
gloved
chest
waist
grouped
gleaming
shoulders

❏ Choose suitable words from around the picture to complete this description.

The alien _____ was a _____, _____
figure. His followers were _____ around him and were
dressed in _____ uniform. No faces were _____
for they were _____ beneath _____ masks with
_____ eyes and _____ horns. We _____
at him _____, not knowing whether he was _____
or _____. His body was _____ in a black, leathery
_____ and his hands were _____. At his
_____ swung a _____, _____ weapon
and from his _____ hung a scaly _____. On his
_____ _____ a badge, _____ the Kerkon
civilization and shaped like a _____ _____, shone
_____, dazzling our _____ eyes.

❏ On a separate sheet of paper design your own Alien Commander and describe
him or her using interesting nouns, adjectives, verbs and adverbs. Use a dictionary
and a thesaurus to help you.

Can you remember?

Mnemonics can help us to remember things. You can use a phrase or rhyme to remember difficult words, lists, spellings and the order of things.
Here is the order of planets from the sun:

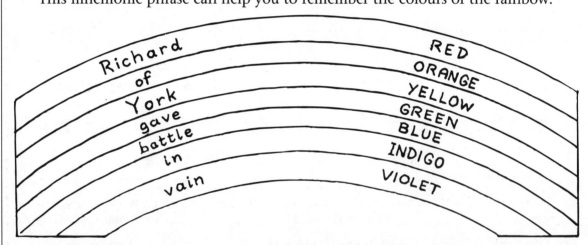

| Mercury | Venus | Earth | Mars | Jupiter | Saturn | Uranus | Neptune | Pluto |

| My | Very | Eager | Mother | Just | Served | Us | New | Potatoes |

❏ Now think of your own mnemonic phrase to help you remember the planets in this order:

M _____ V _____ E _____

M _____ J _____ S _____

U _____ N _____ P _____

This mnemonic phrase can help you to remember the colours of the rainbow:

Richard
of
York
gave
battle
in
vain

RED
ORANGE
YELLOW
GREEN
BLUE
INDIGO
VIOLET

❏ Make up your own mnemonic to help you remember the colours of the rainbow:

R_____ O_____ Y_____ G_____

B_____ I_____ V_____

Here are some difficult words:

(intergalactic)   (meteorite)   (astronomical)

❏ Invent mnemonic phrases or rhymes to help you remember how to spell these words.

Space sense

The words in these sentences have been jumbled up.
❏ Write the correct sentence under each jumbled one.

1 A strong called force gravity tries to pull the back down. rocket

_____

_____

2 A rocket has to have an powerful engine enough to a spacecraft launch into space. _____

_____

_____

3 It is the rocket that second takes stage the spacecraft orbit. into

_____

_____

4 An from astronaut made a space Gemini 4 in 1965. walk

_____

_____

5 When Gemini it used returned to help parachutes it down splash sea. into the _____

_____

_____

❏ Look in encyclopedias or other reference books and find out some more space facts.
❏ Write down the facts in jumbled-up sentences.
❏ Can your friend rearrange them correctly to find out the facts?

photocopiable

Treasure Test 1

❏ Can you spell these words on your empty Treasure Chest sheet? Ask a friend to test you on them. Remember! Look, say, cover, write, check.
Write down each word three times. Every time you get it right, colour in a star in the rocket on the Treasure Chest sheet.

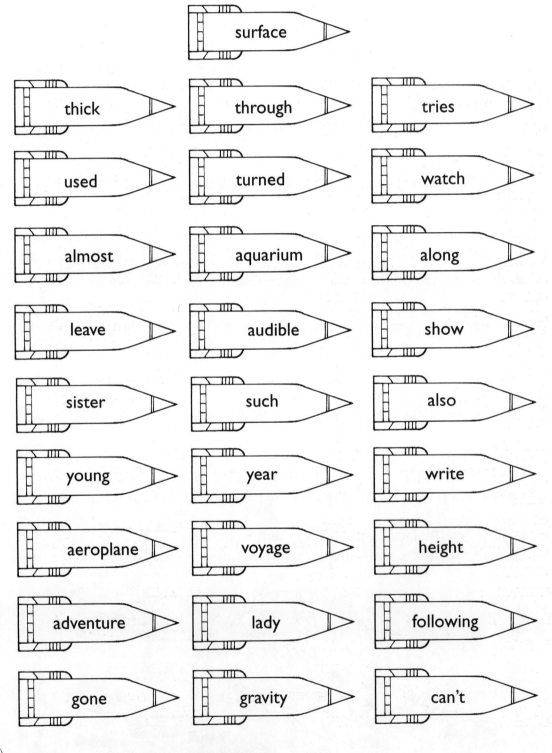

surface

thick   through   tries

used   turned   watch

almost   aquarium   along

leave   audible   show

sister   such   also

young   year   write

aeroplane   voyage   height

adventure   lady   following

gone   gravity   can't

❏ Write any that you find tricky in your Word Explorer.

Treasure Test 2

❑ Can you spell these words on your empty Treasure Chest sheet? Ask a friend to test you on them. Remember! Look, say, cover, write, check.
Write down each word three times. Every time you get it right, colour in a star in the rocket on the Treasure Chest sheet.

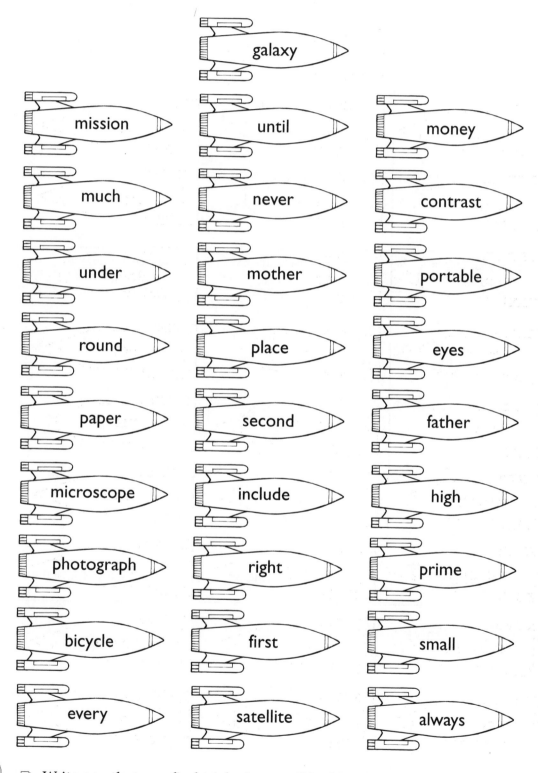

❑ Write any that you find tricky in your Word Explorer.

photocopiable

Look before you leap

Proverbs are wise and traditional sayings that have special meanings.
They are often used to teach a lesson.

❏ Illustrate these proverbs:

1 Don't count your chickens before they're hatched.	**2** Two heads are better than one.	**3** Let sleeping dogs lie.
4 While the cat's away the mice will play.	**5** The early bird catches the worm.	**6** Too many cooks spoil the broth.

❏ What do you think these proverbs mean?

1 _____

2 _____

3 _____

4 _____

5 _____

6 _____

More proverbs

A proverb is a wise, traditional saying used to teach a lesson.

❏ Read the proverbs numbered below and match the numbers to the definitions.

I A fool and his money are soon parted.	**2** A stitch in time saves nine.	**3** Birds of a feather flock together.	**4** Look before you leap.
5 More haste, less speed.	**6** Don't judge a book by its cover.	**7** A bird in the hand is worth two in the bush.	**8** People in glass houses shouldn't throw stones.

Proverb number

☐ Make sure that you know what you are about to do before you act.

☐ What you actually have is worth much more than what you dream of having.

☐ The more hurriedly you try to complete a task, the more likely you are to make careless mistakes which slow you down.

☐ A reckess person can easily be tricked into spending his money on worthless items.

☐ An outward appearance does not necessarily show what is on the inside.

☐ It is foolish to make remarks about the faults of others when you have faults of your own.

☐ Completing a job in good time often saves a lot of work in the long run.

☐ People with similar interests are often drawn together.

Flight

For thousands of years the human race,

Determined to travel into _____,

Has made a range of strange contraptions

In need of subsequent _____.

Icarus and Daedalus, two wily Greeks,

Escaping from their cell in _____,

Flew waxy wings too near the sun

And soon their plan had come _____.

As people raced to see the world

And destinations new _____,

A voracious appetite for flight

Led men to soar to greater _____,

Exploring galaxies unknown,

Unsure of ever reaching _____,

In rockets of complex construction

Which struggled to escape _____.

Soon holidays will be on Mars

And there'll be trips around the _____.

We'll view the next eclipse from space

To satisfy the human _____.

But, wait! Not everyone's agreed

To travel at such height and _____.

There's some feel safer on the _____

Where gravity can't fool around.

C Holloway

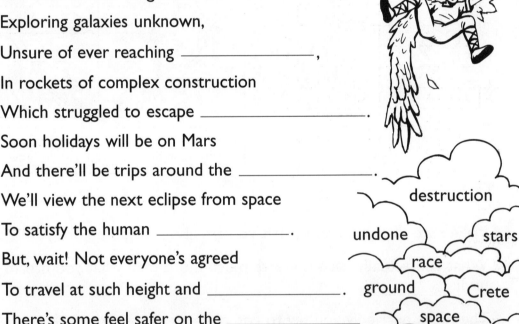

destruction
undone   stars
race
ground   Crete
space
home   height
unfurled
speed
adaptations

❏ Complete the rhyming couplets by using the words in the clouds. Are there any pairs of words which don't quite rhyme?

_____

❏ Write your own short poem on a space theme. First draft it, then edit it and make a final copy.

DICTIONARY

Space chain

The words in this word chain are connected with space travel.

❑ With the help of a dictionary write a clue for each word in the puzzle.

❑ Make up your own word chain on another subject, give the clues to a partner and ask him or her to solve the puzzle.

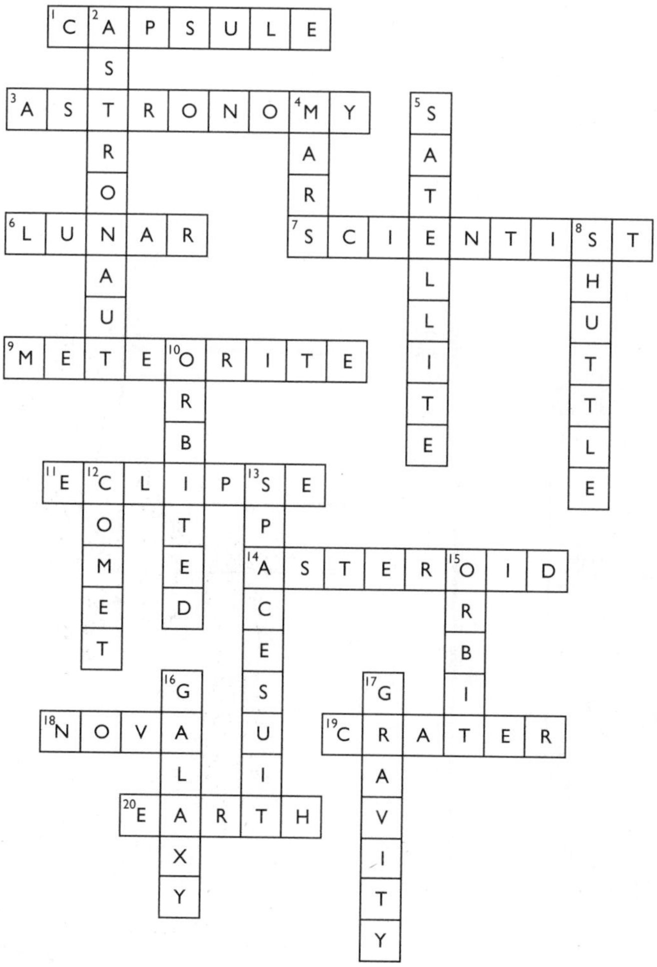
1 CAPSULE
2 ASTRONAUT
3 ASTRONOMY
4 MARS
5 SATELLITE
6 LUNAR
7 SCIENTIST
8 SHUTTLE
9 METEORITE
10 ORBITED
11 ECLIPSE
12 COMET
13 SPACESUIT
14 ASTEROID
15 ORBIT
16 GALAXY
17 GRAVITY
18 NOVA
19 CRATER
20 EARTH

Across

1 ______________________________

____

3 ______________________________

____

6 ______________________________

____

7 ______________________________

____

9 ______________________________

____

11 ______________________________

____

14 ______________________________

____

18 ______________________________

____

19 ______________________________

____

20 ______________________________

____

Down

2 ______________________________

____

4 ______________________________

5 ______________________________

8 ______________________________

10 ______________________________

12 ______________________________

13 ______________________________

15 ______________________________

16 ______________________________

17 ______________________________

Journey into space

These two rockets are about to take off. One is going to Planet Trix**ible** and the other to Planet Trax**able**.

❏ The words in the exhaust fumes have **ible** or **able** missing. Write the completed words on the correct rocket before take off.

10... 9... 8...

To Trixible

To Traxable

imposs-

prob-

revers-

valu-

comfort-

cap-

drink-

sens-

remark-

flex-

respons-

suit-

notice-

terr-

invis-

reason-

fashion-

ed-

lov-

incred-

poss-

reli-

Cut it short

❑ Read this text carefully and summarize its contents in four sentences below.

The solar system

Scientists and astronomers believe that the solar system was created 4600 million years ago. At the centre of the solar system is the Sun. This is the nearest star, being 149.6 million kilometres away. There are nine major planets which are gravitationally bound to the Sun and some of these have satellites. The Earth has one satellite, namely the Moon. The planets all orbit the Sun in the same direction and their journeys form curved paths. Four small planets orbit near to the Sun, their names being Mercury (nearest to the Sun), Venus, Earth and Mars. Jupiter is the fifth and the largest planet. Saturn is famous for its rings which are thought to be made of icy chunks. Uranus is another large planet with a greenish tinge. Neptune is the most distant of the large planets and it has many similarities with Uranus. The planet that is smallest and furthest from the Sun is Pluto. This planet was only recently discovered, in 1930.

Summary

1 _____

2 _____

3 _____

4 _____

❑ Name the planets in the correct order (starting with the planet nearest to the Sun).

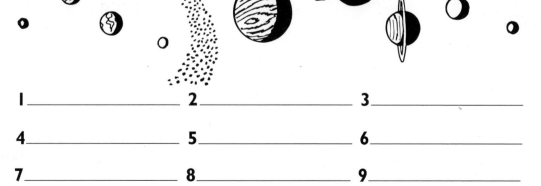

1_____ 2_____ 3_____

4_____ 5_____ 6_____

7_____ 8_____ 9_____

Key words and bullet points

The Earth's biggest plants are trees. The tallest and heaviest are the sequoias that grow in the south-west of the United States of America. Trees continue to grow throughout their lives. They grow taller as twigs at the end of branches grow longer. They grow outwards by adding a layer of new wood underneath the bark, and their roots spread deeper and wider to anchor them securely in the soil.

The roots also supply trees with water and nutrients from the soil. The trunk is a tree's stem. It is lined with tiny tubes in which water from the roots is pumped to all parts of the tree. Branches and twigs support the leaves and allow them to be spread out as much as possible to obtain direct sunlight.

The function of the leaves is to make food by capturing sunlight energy in chlorophyll, the green substance in all plants. They are also the tree's method of "breathing".

There are two types of tree, deciduous and evergreen. Deciduous trees lose their leaves in autumn to protect themselves against cold winter weather. Many evergreen trees have needle-like leaves that have a tough shiny covering that can cope with bitter conditions. These trees keep their leaves for a number of years.

❏ Underline or highlight the key words in this passage that refer to trees.
❏ Represent the main facts in the passage as bullet points.

-
-
-
-
-
-
-
-

The first spacewoman

Valentina Tereshkova was born in Maslennikova, USSR in 1937. When she applied to take part in the Soviet space programme, there seemed to be little hope of her being accepted because she had no experience of space science and some scientists believed space travel would harm the body of a woman.

Valentina had only made her first parachute jump in 1959 but by 1962 she was beginning her training as a cosmonaut. She trained very hard in space technology and amazingly she was chosen to be a member of the crew of Vostok 6 in 1963. The mission was important because when Valentina's craft was in orbit another manned craft, Vostok 5, was launched. This was the first time two manned craft were in orbit at the same time.

Valentina returned to Earth after nearly three days in space. The journey had not harmed her and she was well enough to marry another cosmonaut. Soon after, her daughter, Alyonka, was born in 1964. The birth proved she had suffered no ill-effects in space.

Valentina went on to represent her country and women at conferences all over the world and in 1977 she was awarded the UN Gold Medal of Peace.

❏ Use the passage above to make a timeline and add a note for each date explaining its importance.

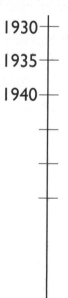

1930
1935
1940

Know your books

❏ Complete the crossword:

Across

4 An information book

6 A book that explains the meanings of words

9 This gives a list of words at the back of a book and explains their meanings

12 This person prints a book and puts it on sale

14 Appears on the front cover of a book

16 This person gets a book ready for publication

17 This tells you when the book was published

19 Library books are arranged in order of the author's one of these

20 A publication that normally has stories and pictures

21 This book contains a list of names in alphabetical order with other information

Down

1 A book that gives you lists of words with similar meanings

2 A book containing maps

3 A publication which contains factual information and is on sale every day

5 A list in alphabetical order at the end of a book with page numbers

7 Letters may be arranged in this order

8 A list of books at the end of a book

10 A business directory: _____ pages

11 A list at the front of a book telling you what's in it

13 A book that people refer to, for information

15 The person who draws pictures in a book

18 The person who writes a book

Let's get active

❏ Change these sentences from the passive to the active form:

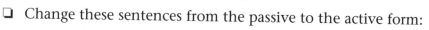

1 Much information about life on Earth was being carried by our spacecraft.

_____

_____

2 This cargo was carefully guarded by four of the crew at all times.

_____

_____

3 As we landed we were welcomed by Commander Crontag, leader of Planet Splontia.

_____

_____

4 The information that we gave to the Splontians was fed into their computer database.

_____

_____

5 We were given specimens of plant life by the Splontians to study back on Earth.

_____

_____

6 The rocket was hit by a giant meteor.

_____

7 Venus was orbited by us for three days.

_____

8 I was given the go-ahead to land by Ground Control.

_____

_____

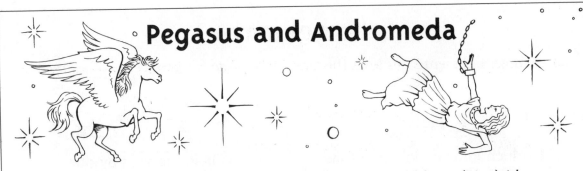

Pegasus and Andromeda

Yesterday was a (nice) day and I thought it would be a (nice) idea to observe the night sky. It was autumn and the sky was (nice) so I could see four (nice) stars making the huge Square of Pegasus. Pegasus was a (nice) flying horse from Greek mythology. These stories are very (nice). A (nice) Greek princess, Andromeda, has a group of (nice) stars named after her just to the left of Pegasus. Andromeda was the daughter of Queen Cassiopeia. The (nice) story tells of how, when a sea monster threatened the country, Andromeda was chosen as a sacrifice. She was rescued by the (nice) hero, Perseus. Now her (nice) galaxy is the closest spiral galaxy to our own (nice) Milky Way.

❑ How many 'nice' words can you replace in the passage? Use a thesaurus to help you choose a better word and try not to use a replacement word more than once. Rewrite the passage below.

_____

_____

_____

_____

_____

_____

_____

_____

_____

_____

_____

_____

_____

_____

Anagrams

❏ Rearrange the anagram to fit the definition. Write the correct word on the line.

1	stomla	=	very nearly _____
2	dtribhay	=	day you were born _____
3	sectolh	=	covers for your body _____
4	endtfifre	=	unalike _____
5	traeh	=	our planet _____
6	hrtafe	=	male parent _____
7	feinrd	=	supporter _____
8	angred	=	cultivated piece of land _____
9	flah	=	either of two equal parts _____
10	ntpomrati	=	of consequence _____
11	pudemj	=	sprang _____
12	ownk	=	be aware _____
13	gilth	=	having little weight _____
14	nymoe	=	coins _____
15	eubnrm	=	count _____

❏ Now make up some of your own using your dictionary.
❏ Try them on a friend.

_____	=	_____	_____
_____	=	_____	_____
_____	=	_____	_____
_____	=	_____	_____
_____	=	_____	_____
_____	=	_____	_____
_____	=	_____	_____
_____	=	_____	_____
_____	=	_____	_____
_____	=	_____	_____

Space puzzles

❏ Find the space words in the wordsearch:

m	c	i	t	c	a	l	a	g	n	t	m	o
c	o	s	m	i	c	o	w	z	u	a	o	t
k	l	s	x	t	g	g	e	a	v	r	t	e
k	u	t	a	a	p	r	n	c	b	r	f	n
j	u	m	l	s	r	o	r	i	a	h	l	a
l	l	a	b	s	r	y	t	p	t	p	i	l
i	x	p	a	t	c	x	o	h	o	b	s	p
y	w	t	s	e	d	t	e	k	c	o	r	h
f	h	a	g	t	v	u	h	f	r	a	t	s

astronaut

rocket

planet

galactic

space

galaxy

cosmic

star

orbit

❏ Here are the answers to a crossword. Now write your own clues!

```
1
E
2
C O N S T E L L A T I O N        4
                    3            N
E                   L        5
C                   I        E A R T H    6
L                   E        P        T
I                            T        I
P                            U        T
7                   8        9        A
S O L A R           L U N A R         N
E                          O
                           C
                           K
                  10
                   S P A C E
                           T
```

Across

2 _____

5 _____

7 _____

8 _____

10 _____

Down

1 _____

3 _____

4 _____

6 _____

9 _____

The phases of the Moon

The Moon takes 29 days to go from new Moon to the next new Moon. As it orbits the Earth diferent parts are lit by the Sun and these chainges are called the Moon's phases.

The phases of the Moon beggin with a new Moon, then the moon becomes a crescent, folowed by a half-Moon, gibbous and a full Moon which is full and rownd. This is called the waxing of the Moon. As the Moon wanes it decreases in size to gibbous, half, crescent to new Moon again.

The lite that we see on the Moon is reflected from the Sun. An eclipse of the Moon happens when the Erth passes beetween the Moon and the Sun causing a shadow upun the Moon's surface. This happens about twice a yeer.

❏ Identify the misspelled words in the passage and write the correct spelling above each incorrect word.

new   crescent   half

gibbous   full   gibbous

half   crescent   new

❏ Why not make a Moon diary for the next 29 days? Draw the Moon at the same time each night and note the 'phases of the Moon'.

Now and then

These children are working at a computer. All the words below are connected with using computer skills.

❏ Find out what each means and write your own definition of each one.

web _____

boot _____

mouse _____

surf _____

keyboard _____

disk _____

program _____

to log _____

monitor _____

screen _____

To children living one hundred years ago, the words above meant something different.

❏ What would children then have understood the words to mean?

web _____

boot _____

mouse _____

surf _____

keyboard _____

disc/disk _____

program(me) _____

to log _____

monitor _____

screen _____

Alien argument

An argument gives a view about something and reasons for that point of view.

STOP PRESS!

Can we be friends with aliens?

Imagine our world has evidence that alien life forms exist on a recently discovered planet. Some people believe it would be a good idea to visit the planet, while others disagree and think it would be wiser not to investigate.

❏ Look at the key points for and against in the table:

for	against
• friendly • good opportunity to study a new/different life form • new technology – advances in medicine • possibility of finding new resources for Earth to use • discover a new philosophy of life – perhaps a more peaceful existence • chance to unite with another planet • new place for human race to explore • chance to learn and share new ideas	• may be hostile • danger of new diseases, viruses, bacteria • alien planet may need Earth's resources; can we afford to share? • lack of understanding about different ways of life • what if Earth has less intelligent life – will our people be exploited? • how can humans be friends with aliens when we never seem to achieve peace among ourselves?

The words and phrases below are often used in arguments.

❏ Choose some of them and use the table (and your own ideas) to write an argument setting out both views *for* and *against* investigating alien life forms.

Introduction (what is the argument about?) *balanced opinion, it is believed, point of view, advantages, disadvantages, agree, disagree*

Development (points of view – for and against) *on the one hand, firstly, also, if, however, furthermore, secondly, although, whereas, on the other hand, the reverse, the opposite, in contrast, in addition*

Conclusion (give your own opinion here) *in conclusion, to sum up, consequently, finally, to summarize, I feel, I believe*

❏ Now write a balanced argument for and against being a child.

Treasure Test 1

❏ Can you spell these words on your empty Treasure Chest sheet? Ask a friend to test you on them. Remember! Look, say, cover, write, check.

Write down each word three times. Every time you get it right, colour in a star in the rocket on the Treasure Chest sheet.

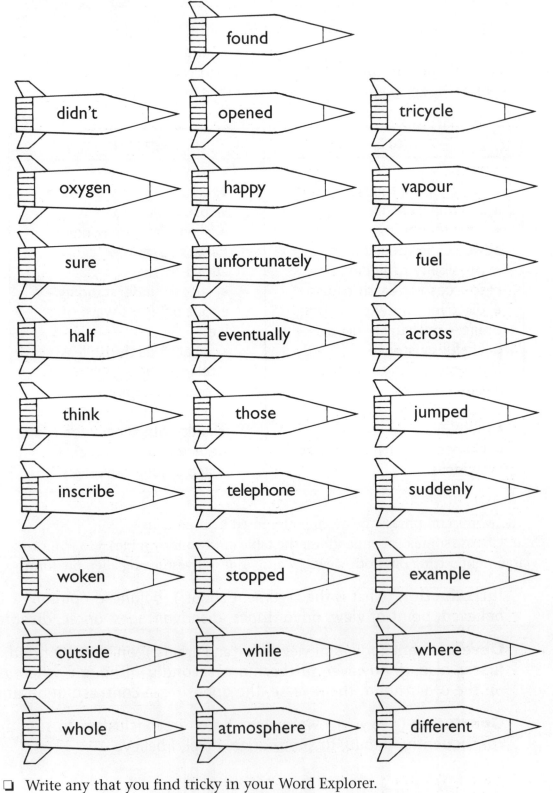

found

didn't | opened | tricycle

oxygen | happy | vapour

sure | unfortunately | fuel

half | eventually | across

think | those | jumped

inscribe | telephone | suddenly

woken | stopped | example

outside | while | where

whole | atmosphere | different

❏ Write any that you find tricky in your Word Explorer.

Treasure Test 2

❏ Can you spell these words on your empty Treasure Chest sheet? Ask a friend to test you on them. Remember! Look, say, cover, write, check.
Write down each word three times. Every time you get it right, colour in a star in the rocket on the Treasure Chest sheet.

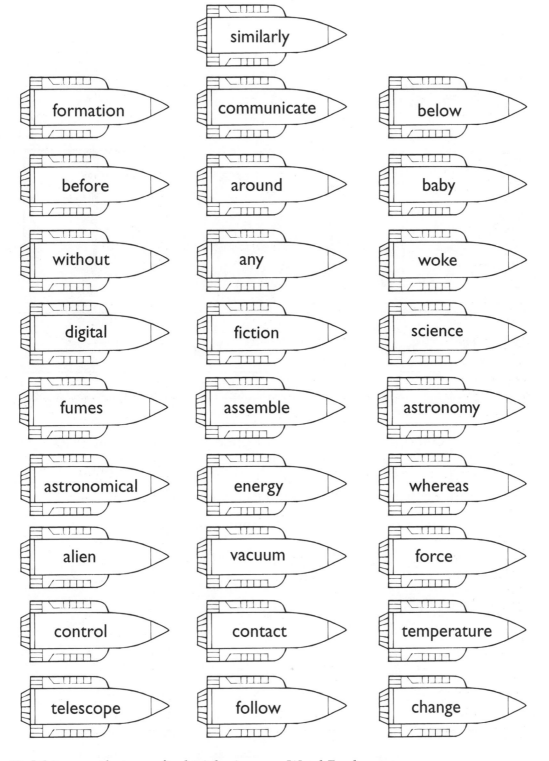

similarly

formation · communicate · below

before · around · baby

without · any · woke

digital · fiction · science

fumes · assemble · astronomy

astronomical · energy · whereas

alien · vacuum · force

control · contact · temperature

telescope · follow · change

❏ Write any that you find tricky in your Word Explorer.

What's your phobia?

A phobia is a fear. The word comes from the Ancient Greek language.

❏ Look at these illustrations and definitions and then, on the grid, 'map' them to the correct phobias. One has been done for you.

Picture number	Phobia	Definition
1	acrophobia	fear of spiders
2	arachnophobia	fear of water
3	xenophobia	fear of open spaces or public places
4	hydrophobia	fear of strangers or foreigners
5	claustrophobia	fear of high places
6	agoraphobia	fear of enclosed places

❏ Describe your own phobia below.

❏ Investigate the names of the phobias above, and then make up a suitable name for your phobia.

_____

_____

_____

_____

_____

Name of phobia: _____

Dictionary delving

❑ Use your dictionary to help you put these words in alphabetical order:

astronaut   astronomical   asteroid
alien   astronomy   atmosphere

galactic   galaxy   gas
global   geology   globe

1 _____
2 _____
3 _____
4 _____
5 _____
6 _____

1 _____
2 _____
3 _____
4 _____
5 _____
6 _____

❑ Write down as many words as you can make from the letters in this word:

C O N S T E L L A T I O N

2 letters	3 letters	4 letters
5 letters	6 letters	7 letters or more

❑ Think of your own space word which has more than nine letters. How many words can you make from the letters in your space word?

A nebula of nouns

A noun is a naming word. There are different types of nouns.

A *common noun* is the name of a person, place or thing, for example **country**, **boy**, **book**.

A *proper noun* is the name of a particular person, place or thing and usually has a capital letter, for example **Jack**, **England**, the **Bible**.

A *collective noun* is the name of a group of things or people, for example a **flock** of sheep.

An *abstract noun* is an idea or feeling, something which cannot be seen or touched, for example **greed**, **love**, **future**.

❏ Decide on which planets these nouns should be placed:

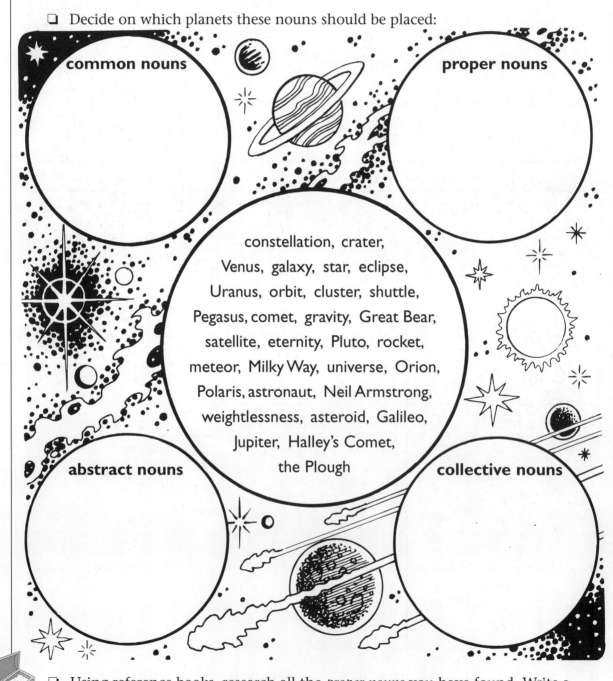

common nouns

proper nouns

constellation, crater, Venus, galaxy, star, eclipse, Uranus, orbit, cluster, shuttle, Pegasus, comet, gravity, Great Bear, satellite, eternity, Pluto, rocket, meteor, Milky Way, universe, Orion, Polaris, astronaut, Neil Armstrong, weightlessness, asteroid, Galileo, Jupiter, Halley's Comet, the Plough

abstract nouns

collective nouns

❏ Using reference books, research all the *proper nouns* you have found. Write a sentence about each of them on the back of this sheet.

Black hole!

❑ Before this black hole implodes, play this word game:

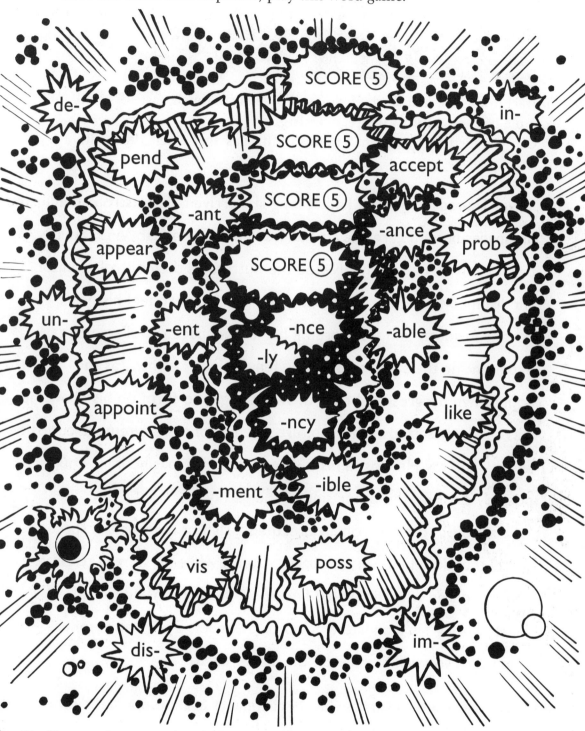

SCORE ⑤

SCORE ⑤

SCORE ⑤

SCORE ⑤

de-   in-

pend   accept

-ant   -ance

appear   prob

un-   -ent   -nce   -able

-ly

appoint   -ncy   like

-ment   -ible

vis   poss

dis-   im-

❑ Choose phonemes from different parts of the black hole to make longer words.
❑ Give a score to every word that you make. For example:

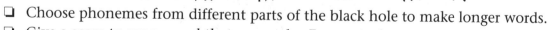

⑤   ⑤   ⑤

dis   appoint   ment   = 15

❑ Who can form the longest list of words?

Alien astronaut

Abstract nouns are nouns which you can't see, hear, touch, taste or smell, for example **bravery**, **knowledge**, **evening**.

❑ Can you identify the abstract nouns in this passage? Circle them with a coloured pencil.

It was Thursday. The day had at long last arrived. The astronaut adjusted his spacesuit with care. Never had he known such fear. With great trepidation he nervously pressed the button on the control monitor and listened for authorization for take-off. He could feel his heart beating furiously and wondered if his fellow space travellers were experiencing the same sensations. Ten… nine… eight… as the countdown progressed, beads of sweat began to form on his brow. He was suddenly seized with a mixture of emotions – excitement, curiosity, anxiety and joy. He closed his eyes and tried to imagine if life could possibly exist on the other side of the galaxy.

"Blast off!" …the astronaut breathed a sigh of relief as the space vessel thundered into outer space. After a while he started to relax and wondered what he would find at his destination. He smiled, remembering his grandfather's words as he left Zorg's atmosphere – "I am sure you will find life on the planet Earth!"

Here are some words which describe the astronaut's qualities and feelings.
❑ Write down the abstract noun from which they are derived.

frightened_____   courageous _____

excited_____   brave _____

apprehensive _____   impatient _____

content _____   hopeful _____

A galaxy of stars

❏ Find the group terms (collective nouns) for these nouns:

Animate

1 a _____ of soldiers   6 a _____ of thieves

2 a _____ of musicians   7 a _____ of buffaloes

3 a _____ of sailors   8 a _____ of puppies

4 a _____ of cattle   9 a _____ of wolves

5 a _____ of birds   10 a _____ of bees

Inanimate

1 a _____ of flowers   6 a _____ of cards

2 a _____ of drawers   7 a _____ of pearls

3 a _____ of steps   8 a _____ of clothes

4 a _____ of bushes   9 a _____ of bananas

5 a _____ of books   10 a _____ of bells

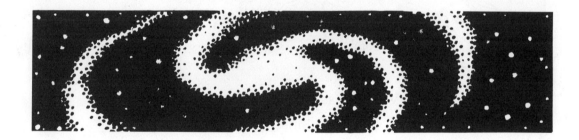

❏ Now finish these examples:

1 a menagerie of _____

2 a mob of _____

3 a regiment of _____

4 a bundle of _____

5 a heap of _____

6 a dozen _____

7 a pair of _____

8 a brace of _____

9 a gross of _____

10 a couple of _____

photocopiable

Glimmering limericks

A limerick is an amusing, five-lined poem with its own special rhyme pattern. Lines one, two and five rhyme together; lines three and four are shorter and rhyme together.

❏ Study the rhyme pattern and rhythm of these two space limericks. Fill in the blanks in the second one and then write one of your own. Use your drafting book and dictionary when planning.

When an astronaut went to the sun,
He was hoping to have lots of fun,
But I've heard a whisper
That he came back crisper
Than bacon that's been overdone!

When an astronaut went to the stars,
He went spinning past Venus and _____.
He said, "Flying through _____
Is undoubtedly 'ace';
It's much better than travelling in cars."

_____
_____
_____
_____
_____

Shooting stars

Assonance is the repetition of vowel sounds to create catchy words or phrases, for example **hot rod** for a souped-up (speedy) car.

❏ Choose the missing words from those at the bottom of the page to complete these words and phrases that all exhibit assonance.

1 ___ and dine

2 dream ___

3 hot ___

4 hog ___

5 horses for ___

6 country ___

7 scally ___

8 ___ and thither

9 hocus ___

10 ___ panky

11 ___ dog

12 ___ 'til you drop

13 flap ___

14 ___ machine

15 ___ nilly

16 hotch ___

17 ___ toity

18 high ___

19 ___ coaster

20 ___ power

wag	hither	flower	team	mean	flyer	courses
willy	hoity	hanky	hot	bumpkin	shop	wash
jack	roller	pocus	potch	pot	wine	

❏ Find the meanings of five of these words/phrases.

The alien plant

❏ Copy out the passage onto a separate sheet of paper and use your thesaurus to substitute the highlighted words with different appropriate words which have a similar meaning.

While **looking around** the unidentified planet, Zeerat had **found** a rather **strange** looking plant. Being **curious**, he had **cautiously** stepped forward to take a closer look. That's when he **became aware** of the **sweet**, intoxicating **smell** being emitted from the plant. He sneezed **abruptly** and felt his eyes **start** to water. Obviously, the pollen had affected him and was making him feel **peculiar**.

He wondered whether to call the others, but he was somehow transfixed by the **strange** beauty of this **entrancing** plant. The petals were **slowly** folding and then unfolding, as if gracefully beckoning to him, and its **gorgeous** flowers were **gently moving** in the **cool** breeze. Zeerat moved yet **closer** to the plant. He had been warned not to get too close to any form of life which he **saw** on this **bleak** planet, but he could not resist edging even closer. This **wonderful** specimen was like a breath of fresh air, a sharp contrast to the **barren** plains which surrounded him.

Nervously, he outstretched his fingers towards the **colourful** array of petals, wondering if they would feel as **beautiful** as they smelled. He **closed** his eyes, inhaled **deeply** as if hypnotized, and prepared himself for the pleasure of delicately touching such a **beautiful** plant.

Little did he know that hundreds of **inquisitive** explorers before him had **fallen** into the same deadly trap…

❏ Write the highlighted words in your Word Explorer.

Fact or fiction?

❑ Write **fact** or **fiction** after each sentence. Use encyclopedias and other reference sources to help you choose.

1 The Earth rotates on its own axis. _____

2 It rotates completely twice every 24 hours. _____

3 The Earth orbits the Moon. _____

4 It takes the Earth 400 days to orbit the Sun. _____

5 The Earth is a satellite of the Sun. _____

6 The Moon is the satellite of the Sun. _____

7 The Moon takes about 29 days to orbit the Earth. _____

8 The Moon's light is a reflection of the Sun's. _____

9 The Sun is a planet. _____

10 The Sun is our nearest star. _____

11 The diameter of the Moon is less than that of the Earth. _____

12 One side of the Moon is always hidden from Earth. _____

13 The 'seas' of the Moon contain water. _____

14 Astronauts have brought back rock from the Moon. _____

15 There are five planets in the solar system. _____

❑ Write five facts about the solar system:

1 _____

2 _____

3 _____

4 _____

5 _____

❑ Write five fictional statements about space:

1 _____

2 _____

3 _____

4 _____

5 _____

Don't say that again!

Tautology is the term for the unnecessary repetition of words or phrases that represent the same idea.

The widow, whose husband had died, was very rich.

❑ In the sentences below, underline the repeated words and phrases and rewrite the sentences without the repetition.

1 The driver, who was fatally injured, died.

_____

2 The annual Christmas fair is held every year in the town hall.

_____

3 The foreigner came from another country.

_____

4 The baby foal trotted beside its mother.

_____

5 Lined up one after another, the people in the queue were served in the post office.

_____

_____

6 The cargo that was being carried on board the ship was mainly sugar.

_____

7 The raw meat couldn't be eaten because it was uncooked.

_____

8 The bungalow was a pretty house and all its rooms were built on one storey.

_____

9 The irate driver looked crossly and glared at the dent in his bumper.

_____

10 Nobody knew who had written the anonymous poem.

_____

Into the future

Past tense	I have flown to Jupiter in the spacecraft.
Present tense	I am flying to Jupiter in the spacecraft.
Future tense	I will fly to Jupiter in the spacecraft.

❏ Rewrite the following passage in the **future** tense.

I have flown over 400,000 miles. I journey through space, faster than the speed of light. I am travelling towards a new planet and am looking forward to finding new life there. As I get closer to the planet, I check my controls to ensure the planet can sustain life. I flick the control switch and send a message back to base to confirm my estimated time of touchdown. I switch the controls to landing mode and approach the planet's surface with caution – and wonder what awaits me.

❏ Imagine you have just landed on the planet. On the back of this sheet, describe what you find there.

photocopiable

Moony metaphors

A metaphor is a figure of speech in which two things are compared. When using a metaphor, we do not say that one thing is like another, we say that it *is* another:

The moon was a silver ball.

❏ Draw a line to match each metaphor to its correct subject.

The aliens	opened their great, yawning mouths on the dark landscape.
Our companion spaceship	were little, rubbery blobs of a jelly-like substance.
Huge craters	was a glittering, crystal ball.
Dark mountains	was a kaleidoscope of magical colours and forms.
A far-off planet	was a silver spinning top hovering far above.
The screen	pointed their cold, eerie fingers upwards.

❏ Write at least two metaphors of your own about the lunar landscape. If you can think of more, write them on the back of this sheet.

1 _____

2 _____

Detailed# Word games

You can move from one word to another by changing one letter at a time. Each time you change a letter, you must spell a new word.

boy ➡ <u>t</u>oy ➡ to<u>p</u>

boy has changed to **top** in 2 moves.

shop ➡ sh<u>i</u>p ➡ <u>c</u>hip ➡ chi<u>n</u>

shop has changed to **chin** in 3 moves.

❑ Change these words in 2 moves:

cup _____ but

rip _____ sit

❑ Change these words in 3 moves:

race _____ _____ palm

slow _____ _____ brow

❑ Change these words in 4 moves:

farm _____ _____ _____ camp

head _____ _____ _____ fear

❑ Think of a word which you can change in 5 moves:

_____ _____ _____ _____ _____

❑ Now solve the anagrams:

1 znooe _____

2 peteumertar _____

3 selpcoeet _____

4 xneopitdei _____

5 rapovu _____

6 otremeite _____

VOCABULARY vocabulary photocopiable

Words within words

❏ Find as many smaller words as you can from the following words.

television   **Score**

vision, son, see

telescope

telegraph

teleprinter

telephoto

telecommunication

❏ What do you think the prefix **tele** means?

_____

photocopiable

Abbreviations and acronyms

An abbreviation is a shortened word.

> telephone – phone   refrigerator – fridge

An abbreviation can also be an acronym, which is where a word is made up from the initial letters of a phrase.

> WHO – World Health Organization
>
> NASA – National Aeronautics and Space Administration

❏ Find out what these abbreviations are short for:

RAC _____

UN _____

VHF _____

FA _____

DIY _____

AAA _____

The following passage contains abbreviated words.

❏ On a separate sheet, rewrite the passage, writing the abbreviations in full.

I rang the **RSPB** yesterday to find out more about a species of bird I couldn't identify. I spoke to a famous man, Dr Stevens, who has worked with a variety of birds in **LA** in the **USA**. He asked me to write to him **asap** and he said that he would send me some details in the post as long as I include an **sae**. I have also written to the **RSPCA** to see if they can send me any other relevant information. I intend to send my letter tomorrow and I shall mark it **FAO** Dr Stevens. I think I might add a **PS** at the end of the letter telling him how good I thought his recent article was in the **FT** newspaper. Dr Stevens will also be on the radio tomorrow at 7pm on the *Bird Talk* programme. I feel really fortunate to have spoken to such a famous **VIP**!

So, you want to be an astronaut

❑ Tick the qualities you think are essential to be an astronaut.

The astronaut should be:

1 Healthy in body and mind ☐

2 Good-looking and fashionable ☐

3 Cheerful when in difficult situations ☐

4 Able to think quickly and solve problems independently ☐

5 A fussy eater who is often ill ☐

6 Argumentative and hot-tempered ☐

7 Responsible and trustworthy ☐

8 Able to sit still for long periods ☐

9 A good writer ☐

10 Unable to take advice ☐

11 A fan of space fiction like *Star Trek* ☐

12 A man ☐

13 Good at science and mathematics ☐

14 Able to recover quickly from air-sickness ☐

15 Lonely when on their own ☐

16 Colour-blind ☐

17 Afraid of heights ☐

18 Calm in an emergency ☐

19 Physically strong ☐

20 Intelligent and hard-working ☐

❑ Find as many adjectives as you can to describe an astronaut like Neil Armstrong. Use a thesaurus.

A safe landing

❏ Look carefully at this picture before you write a description of the scene. Write a draft on a separate sheet of paper first. Concentrate on including *suitable adjectives* to make your account as vivid and lively as possible.

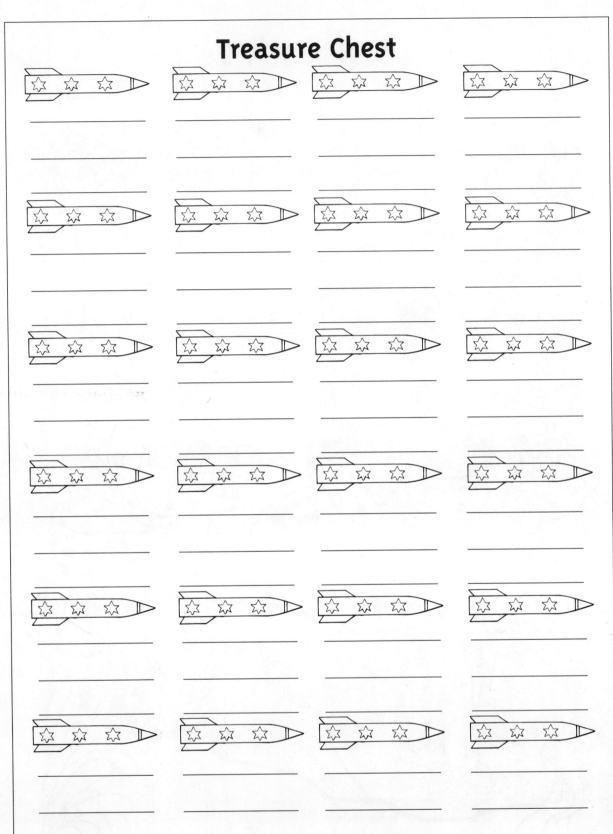

Treasure Chest

photocopiable